I'm Scared

5 easy steps
for child anxiety

MEG WARDLAW

PRAISE FOR *I'M SCARED*

This book is such an easy-to-read, straight-forward book with lots of tips and strategies to help parents in those tricky situations. It will be welcomed by parents as an invaluable reference.

Dr Vanessa Wing-Quay, Clinical Psychologist

This is an invaluable guide for parents and so accessible for anyone struggling with an anxious child. What a great book!

Julie Postance, Author

Meg's approachable nature alongside extensive clinical experience comes through clearly in the numerous case examples, and recommendations to parents.

Dr Sonja Skocic, Clinical Psychologist

Wise words of wisdom, easily understood, with practical strategies to cope with an anxious child. A "must have" resource for parents and carers in this modern world.

Lu Smith, Parent

A wonderful resource for families. This is an evidenced-based resource, but what really sets this book apart is the author's clinical experience and the clear, easy-to-use approach. Parents will find the practical examples are authentic and will resonate on a personal level for many people.

Recommendations will provide families with an easy-to-use roadmap through the often-tumultuous journey of supporting your child's anxiety.

In many ways it is a book that is a must-read for all parents as it speaks to one of the fundamental bedrocks of parenting — the ability to tune into and understand your child's psychological experiences.

Colin McMeekin, Psychologist

This is such a great book, and one that is sorely necessary in a world where anxiety, especially in children and young people, is on the rise. The easy-to-understand language means it will be accessible to socio-economic backgrounds, education levels, and those with English as a second language (which is a major deal considering anxiety has no borders or bounds).

Amanda Spedding, Author

What a great resource for parents and carers of anxious children! The easy-to-read steps make a great starting point for any parent or carer dealing with this complex issue.

Pam Scott, Family Therapist

For parents and carers of anxious children and young people, this book is an invaluable parenting resource. In fact, all parents would benefit from reading this book.

The many case examples, suggested strategies and proposed parent-child conversations are presented in an easy to understand, engaging and supportive style that parents and carers will readily relate too.

For parents who are struggling to help their anxious child cope with worries and navigate life's experiences, this book is a "must read".

Robyn Peel, Social Worker

Published in Australia by
Growing Stronger Publishing

27 Little Myers St Geelong Vic Australia
PO Box 3038 Geelong VIC Australia 3220
admin@growingstronger.com.au
www.growingstronger.com.au

First published in Australia 2019

Copyright © Meg Wardlaw 2019

All rights reserved. No part of this publication may be reproduced, stored in a retrieval system, or transmitted, in any form or by any means without the prior written permission of the publisher, nor be otherwise circulated in any form of binding or cover other than that in which it is published and without a similar condition being imposed on the subsequent purchaser.

National Library of Australia Cataloguing in Publication entry

A catalogue record for this book is available from the National Library of Australia

Creator: Wardlaw, Meg, author.

Title: I'm Scared: 5 easy steps for child anxiety / Meg Wardlaw.

ISBN: 978-0-6480916-3-9 (paperback)

Subjects: Anxiety-Treatment.
Stress in children-Prevention.
Stress in children-Treatment.
Anxiety in children-Treatment.
Stress management for children.
Parenting.

Cover photography by Shutterstock® The cover image is for illustrative purposes only, and any person featuring is a model

Cover layout and design by Aksaramantra and Sophie White
Illustrations by Paul Cox
Book typesetting by Sophie White

Printed by Kindle Direct Publishing

Disclaimer

All care has been taken in the preparation of the information herein, but no responsibility can be accepted by the publisher or author for any damages resulting from the misinterpretation of this work. All contact details given in this book were current at the time of publication, but are subject to change.

The advice given in this book is based on the experience of the individuals. Professionals should be consulted for individual problems. The author and publisher shall not be responsible for any person with regard to any loss or damage caused directly or indirectly by the information in this book.

DISCLAIMER

Even though Meg Wardlaw is a psychologist this book is in no way aimed to give specific psychological advice. The whole book is designed to give a general overview of what a parent can try to ease anxiety. But every child is different, so these strategies may assist some children but not others.

Please remember these strategies are general in nature, and not designed to be a one-size-fits-all, as anxiety varies greatly from child to child. They may not apply or be successful for all children.

It is very important to consult a health-care practitioner (eg. psychologist, social worker, counsellor) if your child does not want to engage, or if there seems to be no progress.

Finally, all the case studies in this book are combined examples of real situations with fictitious names, so no child can be identified.

I'm Scared

ABOUT THE AUTHOR

Meg Wardlaw is an experienced psychologist who has worked for over 25 years in the public health and education fields, as well as in private practice. She currently runs a very successful and busy private practice for children and young adults.

As she is frustrated by not being able to provide service to all the people requesting advice, she decided to write a book to help parents of anxious children.

Meg has two young-adult sons, and loves to spend time with her family and friends. When not working, she enjoys going to the gym and going for walks.

A keen theatre-goer, Meg is on the board of Back to Back Theatre, an internationally-renowned theatre group. Based in Geelong, it creates innovative and creative performance by people with so-called disabilities. Check them out at www.backtobacktheatre.com

Meg lives in South-Western Victoria, Australia, which is home to the Great Ocean Road, and its glorious beaches.

I'm Scared

This book is dedicated to my sons, Tom and Pat, who have generously tolerated "Mum's work" encroaching on their lives.

It is also dedicated to all my clients, who have helped me to better understand their experiences.

I'm Scared

CONTENTS

Foreword	1
Introduction	3
STEP ONE: What is this thing called anxiety?	7
STEP TWO: Understanding the physical effects of anxiety	35
STEP THREE: Linking thoughts and feelings	69
STEP FOUR: Pushing through	95
STEP FIVE: Building resilience and further skills	115
What else can I do?	161
Appendix	171
Useful resources	175
Acknowledgements	183

I'm Scared

FOREWORD

It has been my great pleasure to know Meg since we first met as students studying psychology together at the University of Melbourne, well over 30 years ago. I am delighted to be writing this foreword.

Meg's caring nature, compassion, and empathy are her defining qualities and have been present in her ongoing work with families and children. These qualities are apparent in this book, and in its aim to enable parents to feel they can cope and support their child during the stressful times.

Childhood is supposed to be a happy and carefree time, but for a significant and increasing number of Australian children, the presence of anxiety interferes. While some anxiety and fears in children is normal, there are times this emotion can become debilitating. Meg's book aims to give parents confidence to intervene and take control early. Adults with anxiety often recall *"This is the way I have always been"*, Meg's book gives parents an opportunity to alter this trajectory.

This book is easy-to-read and will be of benefit to parents and carers. Many people just don't have access to a psychologist, whether it be for financial reasons, or because of their geographical location. Now, this book gives everyone a place to start. As anxiety seems to be on the rise world-wide, I am so thrilled this resource has become available.

Elizabeth Williams
Bachelor of Arts (Honours), Master of Educational Psychology, University of Melbourne

I'm Scared

INTRODUCTION

This book had to be written. Not because I would like to be an author; I don't really have those aspirations. Rather, because so many parents are struggling with anxious children. As the world becomes more stressful, and as we live with varying degrees of terrorism, the need for strategies grows. There are lots of other good books for anxious children, and yet, I felt this book was needed.

I often talk to students in high school about choosing between 'quick- and-dirty' tasks — which are the short/sharp homework tasks versus the long, drawn-out assignments that require more thinking. This book is like the quick-and-dirty tasks. It gives some explanation but is generally simplistic in nature.

The purpose of this book is to provide ideas and strategies for parents who are struggling with very difficult situations that you can apply immediately. Hopefully, before long, you will notice a difference in your child.

From my extensive experience as a psychologist in public health and private practice, I have watched the rise in mental health issues for many children and young people. Recent studies have suggested anxiety disorders are increasing as a world-wide phenomenon.

At the much-appreciated urging of Dr Sonja Skocic, clinical psychologist, I present to you some preliminary 'how to's' for the anguished parent or carer. My aim is to present the key information without too much reading.

But an important point first, my aim is for you as the parent or carer to read the book first, and then return to the book to use the speech bubbles that explain things to your child.

You may like to start by saying something like:

> We are going to start trying to help you deal with the worries you are having. But we will just do a little bit at a time. It should be fun doing it together.
>
> I will try to understand a bit more about how anxiety or worries work, and we can make some plans about the best way to deal with them.
>
> First, I need to understand what is going on by reading this book and then we will get to work.

Throughout the book, I have included speech bubbles that give you — as the parent or carer — an idea of what to say. It will not matter whether you use the term anxiety, worries, Mr Irrits, or something else to describe the anxiety. All these terms are fine to use. The main thing is that you communicate what to do when these awful feelings strike.

You will need to spend time reading the book, and then set aside some short 20 to 30-minute sessions with your child to absorb the information and discuss it.

Please do not try to complete the sessions in one sitting. If you try to do one session with your child full-bore from start to finish, it will not work. Children need time to think about each step and each piece of information.

While it might seem simplistic in parts, this book is designed for easy conversation with children primarily aged between 7-12 years. Of course, these are the preliminary steps to try, and if there is no improvement, professional support and guidance should be sought.

It is important for me to highlight that even though the case examples may seem familiar, they are drawn from a collective array of experiences. For confidentiality, no real clients' names or situations have been used.

If you feel like your experience is presented on the page, it is probably just another reminder of how many people are suffering just like you!

But first, four important things to know about this book:

1. By reading this book first, before starting work with your child, you get to know how scary anxiety can be. By understanding what your child is feeling, it can make it easier to work on the problem.

2. Take one step at a time. It will not work if you try to do it all at once. Don't try to read it all or do it all in one go. It won't work!

3. Set aside a regular time, preferably each week to work on these steps. You are giving your child the message: This is important, and YOU are important to me.

4. Please, please, please do not just read out 'the words' (in speech bubbles) for your children. It is important that you know and understand the reasons for the words.

STEP ONE

What is this thing called anxiety?

WHAT IS THIS THING CALLED ANXIETY?

The first step is getting to know how anxiety affects us. Not just so that you know how it feels, that's important too, but we need to really understand how it feels for children. Then we can work out what to do to help. Children need to know that this is not just 'freaky me', this happens to lots of people — young and old, boys and girls.

I find anxiety occurs in the nicest of people. The sufferers can be greatly concerned about the well-being of other children or adults around them, but the worries grow.

It is important to convey this message to children to help build a healthy self-esteem. The message they need to tell themselves is: "I am not freaky. And I am a nice person." Already it doesn't seem so bad.

Also, there are many children suffering from anxiety, but no one likes to talk about it. Children don't like to admit they are struggling, and parents or carers are sometimes ashamed or embarrassed to admit it to friends and family.

Prevalence rates are inconsistent but the National Institute of Mental Health (USA) has suggested up to 30% of young people aged 13-18 years will have an experience of anxiety symptoms, with around 8% experiencing a 'severe' anxiety disorder.

> *Olivia had appeared to be a happy and confident five-year-old when she started school. She loved school and loved her teacher. But one day she started to become reluctant to attend school. Her grandmother, her carer, was concerned by this change in attitude, and provided a special after-school snack, so they could 'wonder' about it together.*
>
> *It turned out Olivia's friend had told her of a dog that attacked someone on the way to school. Olivia's grandmother promised to investigate and contacted the school the following day. The school reported there had been no incidents of a dog bite on the way to school, but they were aware of one student who had been bitten by his bunny while trying to feed it.*
>
> *Olivia's grandmother and Olivia remarked on how much the message had changed as it got passed on, and realised there had never been a threat at all.*

What is anxiety?

If you have watched your child melt-down from anxiety, you know how distressing this experience is. Not just for your child, but for you as the parent or carer as well.

If you have battled with a child to get them to school, you know the feeling 'I've done my day's work already!'

WHAT TO SAY

The person who wrote this book has worked out that this worry stuff happens all the time. Maybe three or four kids from your class have it.

She thinks it happens to lots of nice, kind people.

But you know what? Even though lots of people have it, no one talks about it. Worried people don't like to tell others how worried they are, just in case they seem stupid!

While all children experience some symptoms of anxiety, such as butterflies in the stomach or a dry mouth, it is not considered a problem until it prevents your child from engaging in and enjoying everyday life.

Step One: What is this thing called anxiety?

> *Sally is nine years old and lives at home with her loving parents and two sisters. Every night as she goes to bed she begins to feel anxious about school the next day. She spends much of her time before bed telling her parents how sick she is feeling. By the morning, her body is shaking, she has stomach pains and she is feeling dry in the mouth.*
>
> *She insists she is sick and needs to stay home. She tries stalling tactics, hiding under the covers, and even holding onto the bed so she isn't dragged to the shower. It is a nightmare experience for everyone!*
>
> *Everyone hopes the next day will be better. But, it isn't.*
>
> *Her sisters demand to be taken to school before her. Her parents, who usually take turns taking the children to school, secretly hope they can pass the chore on to the other, with excuses like, "I have to be at work early".*
>
> *And Sally just keeps crying and screaming all the way to school.*

This is just one picture of anxiety. Sally's anxiety is overwhelming and interfering with her everyday life, particularly attending school.

> **WHAT TO SAY**
>
> Everyone has worries.
>
> Sometimes they are big. Sometimes they are small.
>
> But if they get in the way of life, then it's a problem. And we need to do something about it.

How common is anxiety?

Recent Australian research has suggested that around 5-7% of children and young people meet the criteria for what is technically called an anxiety disorder *(Report on the Second Australian Child and Adolescent Survey of Mental Health and Wellbeing, August 2015)*. According to this comprehensive research, boys and girls tend to get anxiety disorders at an equal rate. It is not just a 'girl thing', as is sometimes thought.

From this, we can see anxiety disorders are very common, and anxiety symptoms even more so. More and more studies across the world are being conducted to review child mental health issues.

Step One: What is this thing called anxiety?

In this book, I will not make a distinction between anxiety and anxiety disorders. If your child is experiencing intense anxiety, I hope by following these steps you will see a change in his or her ability to cope with the world.

I'm Scared

As a tall Year-5 student, adults expected a lot of Thomas. Whenever adults came to ask Thomas and his friends for directions to the school office, they would always turn to Thomas.

The trouble was Thomas was not confident when speaking to adults. He would mumble, blush, and sometimes found no words would come out. His friends were astonished. Thomas usually had no difficulty telling them what to do, or how to do it.

As the friends continued to play near the school entrance, Thomas tried to find different ways to avoid the adults. He would suggest playing in alternative areas. He was on constant watch for strangers entering the school, and if anyone came near him he would quickly excuse himself and head for the toilets.

If he happened to meet an adult, and this rarely happened, he learned the handy comment: "I'm not sure. What do you think, Andy?"

Thomas never mentioned these difficulties at home, and it was a huge surprise to his mother when she overheard the back-seat conversation about the many different avenues Thomas had to avoid any conversation with visitors to the school.

When quizzed about it later, Thomas admitted he did not like being asked questions to which he did not know the answer. His mother pointed out that he was a master of maps and navigation, and she thought he could direct *anyone anywhere.* She suggested this was more about confidence than not knowing the answer.

She congratulated Thomas on being so clever as to come up with a standard line of, "I'm not sure. What do you think, Andy?" But suggested he could be equally clever as to come up with a rehearsed comment about the location of the office from any point in the school.

His mother insisted, much to Thomas' annoyance, that they practise one afternoon after school. She stood in ten different locations, and asked Thomas for directions. She recorded each command on her phone and then encouraged Thomas to write them out and learn them. It was all very irritating for Thomas, especially as he could see no point to it!

But, suddenly the crisis of confidence was gone. Thomas became more and more confident in giving directions and, ultimately, he was made school greeter at the gate for all official functions.

Sometimes children don't realise their anxiety is evident to others. Sometimes they don't realise the underlying difficulty or the reason for the worries. Thomas' mother was lucky enough to hear the back-seat conversation, but sometimes it is only by careful coaxing or drawing-out that the reason for the behaviour becomes apparent.

Why does anxiety occur?

No one really knows why anxieties occur, although sometimes it can come from a traumatic incident, or accident. Sometimes, the tendency for anxiety runs in families, and sometimes it is associated with neurological conditions such as an Autism Spectrum Disorder.

Anxiety can also result from an everyday experience.

> *Little Paddy was a two-year-old toddler. He loved going to the beach. He loved the sand, the waves, and building sand-castles. It was his slice of heaven in a very busy world.*
>
> *One day as his parents watched him in the water he got knocked down by a sudden big wave that hit him from behind. Even though his parents pulled him up quickly, he had swallowed some water and came up coughing and spluttering.*
>
> *From that moment, he became terrified of the ocean and the beach. It was no longer his favourite place to go, and he would prefer to stay at home and do puzzles rather than head for the beach.*
>
> *Slowly and gently his parents coaxed him back to the beach and taught him to enjoy making sand-castles again. But, it took the whole summer for him to become confident enough to return to the shallows.*

Anxiety can occur at any age, but anxiety can increase as a child grows older, so it becomes particularly important to address early on.

There are some key stages for children to experience anxiety, and these are developmentally appropriate. The most prominent are:

- A baby becomes shy or anxious when around strangers in the first year of life
- A toddler becomes scared of thunderstorms, the dark, and nightmares
- Around 5-7 years, a fear of death of parents, natural disasters, and anxiety centred on school performance may develop
- In adolescence, worries about being rejected by peers may emerge

Anxiety sometimes becomes more evident around the age of seven. This seems to coincide with a child starting to use logic to solve problems. They understand that parents or carers cannot always protect them from the world. The fairy stories of "they lived happily ever after" don't always apply in real life, and they are starting to realise it!

Suddenly, the child may start to think, *What's stopping Mum or Dad or my carers from getting killed?* And... *Where's my guarantee when they say it won't happen?* Very scary thoughts indeed.

I'm Scared

At four years of age, Jack was a proud kindergarten boy. He was proud of being a 'grown-up' boy, and proud of all the things he was learning to do at kindergarten.

But at night, everything changed. Jack was scared of monsters in his bedroom. He told his father he could see the monsters in the dark and he could hear them in the night-time. Sometimes they made loud noises, sometimes they made tiny rattling sounds.

Jack's lack of sleep was affecting his learning, and he was often grumpy. His parents were beginning to despair. They argued with Jack that monsters didn't exist. They argued that there was nothing there. But Jack would not and could not be convinced.

Jack's father got children's books from the library about monsters in the dark. Some showed pictures of clothes looking like monsters, some showed all houses have noises in the night-time.

Jack and his Dad developed a game in which they had to think of how many things could make noises at night. First, there were obvious ones, like the dog and cat. Others were less obvious, like the refrigerator and the noise of the wooden cladding on the house moving in the wind.

Jack would often feel uncomfortable about the thoughts of monsters during the night and would often need his father to lie with him when he went to bed. But by having some reasons for the noises in his house, he managed to get to sleep. At least on some nights!

Younger children often have difficulty understanding the difference between what is real and what is imagined.

The famous psychologist, Jean Piaget, described the cognitive developmental stages of children. He highlighted the stage of concrete operations, which occurs around the ages of 7-11 years, in which children can start to use logical thoughts when thinking about the world.

Clearly, Jack has not yet reached this stage, but it is still important for his father to persuade Jack there are no monsters. Explaining why Dad thinks there are no monsters may help him to stay calmer.

WHAT TO SAY

No one knows why some people have more worries than others. Sometimes it runs in families. Sometimes it comes from a scary experience.

Sometimes it happens when you are always being told "Watch out for that!" If people say "watch out!" over and over, that can make you even more scared.

But a lot of the time we just don't know where it has come from.

Why does it feel like anxiety is more common?

The power of social media

As the world has contracted through social media and Internet access, we feel our neighbours across the nation — and even internationally — have grown closer. If we want to see the little town we were born in, even though it is hundreds of kilometres away, we can check it out on Google Earth.

If we want to see what the rebels are saying during a national uprising, we can find out through Reddit, Twitter or Facebook or any other avenue of social media. If we want to know what everyone is thinking about a certain issue, we can find out immediately.

Suddenly the world has shrunk. Suddenly our neighbours are not those people next door but the people we play games with, who happen to live on the other side of the world. In fact, we may not even know our neighbours next door.

Suddenly when there is a crisis or disaster somewhere, it is not a thousand miles away, it feels like it is on our doorstep. And we may be concerned for our Facebook friends and associates, just as much as we are for our 'real' friends and family.

How much more is there to worry about, too, when we know the rules have changed. Not only do we have newspapers and television programs telling us there is disaster everywhere, but we know the 'bad guys' are changing the rules and finding new ways to commit atrocities. Furthermore, the bad guys seem to be winning!

Even if you are protecting your children from the news, you may be conveying the above in conversation with others, and by driving past news billboards. The world has become a whole lot scarier! Is it any wonder the rates of anxiety for children and young people are rising?

And indeed, anxiety is becoming a topic of discussion. Much more than it had previously. Professor Barbara Milrod from the Medical College, Cornell University is a child and adolescent psychiatrist and psychoanalyst with expertise in anxiety disorders. She described in *The Conversation*, that after the US 2016 election, and the general political upheaval that accompanied it, medical professionals across the country had observed an 'increase in agitation and anxiety' among their young patients.

I'm Scared

Grace was an enthusiastic Year 6 student. She was diligent and conscientious and was always keen to help the teacher in the classroom.

At parent-teacher interviews Grace's parents were regularly told, "If only I had a class full of Graces!"

As a bright girl, Grace took a keen interest in the world around her. She was fascinated by newsfeeds and Facebook posts, and was always keen to see what her friends were doing on the various social media sites.

However, as Grace became more aware of the political turmoil around her, she started to become scared by discussion of war breaking out. Her fears began to overwhelm her.

She would stay close to her teacher and friends at school, and that puzzled them. She would not leave her parents' side at home, even when they were just going to the garage. Whereas in the past she would happily stay home alone, now she was always insistent she would travel with her parents wherever they were going.

Grace's parents were quite overcome by this behaviour. Their fiercely independent daughter had become totally reliant on them. She wouldn't even walk down the hallway to her bedroom by herself.

In speaking with Grace, her parents became aware she had become terrified of nuclear warfare. She watched the news, she knew what the political leaders were saying.

> *She was terrified. Something awful was going to happen, and in her mind it was going to happen at any minute.*
>
> *Once they realised the torture Grace was putting herself through, her parents started to explain some important facts about the world. Safeguards had been put in place by the politicians, even if they seemed full of dangerous talk. And they were using 'back channels' to help calm the situation. Even though they didn't know what was happening, it was important to explain steps were being taken to keep things calm.*
>
> *They helped her to understand that nuclear disaster was not imminent, and Grace and her friends would continue to be safe.*

But social media is not just a source of gaining information about impending disasters across the world, it is also a powerful source of comparison. Sites such as Instagram, Snapchat and Facebook can all demonstrate friends and family who appear to be doing 'better'. Whether 'better' is from buying things or looking more attractive doesn't matter, the fear of not making the grade grows. And so does anxiety.

Anxiety can be crippling

Anxiety disorders can be debilitating and interfere with everyday life. That's when it becomes a problem.

It is a problem if a child:

- Can't do everyday activities
- Can't behave like his or her peers
- Can't perform at his/her best, or close to his/her best
- Finds it is interfering with his/her life

> Anna has a close group of friends. They love catching up together. They hang out at weekends, go shopping together, and have sleepovers.
>
> Anna is happy to have friends sleep over at her place but cannot sleep at friends' houses. Sadly, even though she is 12 years old she needs to leave before lights out because of her fear of sleeping in a stranger's house. She always finds an excuse such as her parents don't like her to be away from home.
>
> Her friends always ask why her parents can't just let her come for a sleepover. She laughs it off but doesn't explain.

Although a child's age affects what they can tolerate, if Anna's peers can manage the sleepover without problems, then the anxiety is interfering with her everyday life. The shame and embarrassment she feels are also clues that she has some work to do. Probably the first step is for Anna to tell her friends she is struggling so they can support her in the steps ahead.

> *At nine years of age, Jeremy has a fear of spiders. So do many of his friends.*
>
> *But for Jeremy, the fear is overwhelming.*
>
> *He searches his bed before he gets into it. He stares at the ceilings and walls as he goes to sleep, searching for spiders. Usually he doesn't get to sleep until around midnight. By the time he wakes up, he is exhausted for the day.*

These anxieties mean that Jeremy is not getting the sleep necessary for a child his age. He is spending his entire days on a mission searching for the enemy — the spider. Poor young fellow is exhausted! This is another example of the worry interfering with everyday life.

A touch of anxiety

> Johnny feels worried whenever he has a test. He particularly dislikes having surprise tests.

Most children don't like having tests, and they may experience a few butterflies, especially when given a surprise test for which they have not prepared. That's okay. If most children would feel worried by the event and Johnny is not losing sleep, then it is a normal part of growing up, and facing up to the worry is a part of developing resilience.

> Cecilia gets butterflies every time she participates in a swimming race. Fortunately, she swims good times, and is hoping to make the national team next year.
>
> But she is worried the fear will overwhelm her, and make her swim poorly.

Sometimes anxiety can be helpful, and it can actually cause people to perform at their best. Most athletes and swimmers have had the experience of adrenalin pumping before a race. A touch of anxiety can be a most useful thing! A touch of anxiety can help to build resilience and make children stronger.

WHAT TO SAY

Anxiety can sometimes help people to do things better and make them feel stronger. So we can have good anxiety as well as bad anxiety.

Anxiety is only bad if it stops us from doing the normal things in life.

But if it is starting to take over your life, we need to do something about it.

Why can't they just get over it?

Often parents or carers are tempted to tell their children to harden up, or to tough it out. Unfortunately, this is not helpful if the child is struggling with anxiety.

> *Declan's grandmother cared for him following a tragic car accident in which his parents were killed.*
>
> *Eight-year-old Declan was terrified when crossing the street, and his grandmother encouraged him to get on with living with some tough love.*
>
> *Unfortunately, it was not until one year later that she sought help for Declan, as the tough love had not worked. Poor Declan had been a very distressed young lad for a very long twelve months.*

It is more helpful to give children strategies and to support them through the challenges they face, than expecting them to tough it out and get over it. By understanding the anxiety, you can help them to build life-long skills. By understanding anxiety, you can help them to cope with new situations and challenges in life.

Often it is tempting to think children, or young people, have much tougher times ahead. Sometimes managing anxiety can be the biggest challenge in a person's life, no matter their age!

Remember, it isn't helpful to tell them: "You are going to have to deal with worse things than this in your life." Because to them, it sure feels like this is as bad as it can get.

> **WHAT TO SAY**
>
> **I know feeling like this is really, really hard. Worries can be like that.**
>
> **Sometimes, getting over worries can be the hardest thing someone does in their whole life. It doesn't matter whether they are young or old. But once you have beaten them, you are ready for anything!**

Understanding your own anxiety

Sometimes a parent or carer's own anxiety impacts on the child. If you are highlighting dangers to your child at every step, they can begin to learn the world is a very dangerous place. As they become aware of the dangers, their worries increase.

> *Felicity knew about anxiety. She had experienced it as a child and knew only too well what Joey was going through. She was a caring, nurturing mother, and of course she pointed out the dangers as they walked around the neighbourhood.*
>
> *As she walked with Joey, she would recite: "Watch out for that uneven ground, watch out for that stray dog, watch out for that car reversing."*
>
> *As Joey grew older, he added plenty more worries to the list. And so, the big list of worries grew, and he grew more and more anxious every day.*

In one interesting study Pass, Mastroyannopoulou, Coker, Murray and Dodd, (2017), studied the language mothers used when speaking to their children starting school. The authors found that anxious mothers were more likely to mention at least one anxiety-related word in conversation, and to show clear or consistent negative thoughts when speaking with their children about school.

This is a reminder to us all that we pass on our own anxiety to our children and young people with the words we use.

It seems that it is not just through genetics that we can pass on worries, but we can also convey our anxiety in what we do and what we say. Another reason to worry? No, just another reason to think about the language we use when speaking to children and young people.

Different types of anxiety

There are many different types of anxiety, but only general anxiety will be discussed here. The standard psychiatric tool for diagnosis of disorders (DSM-V) used by psychologists and psychiatrists around the world, outlines many different types of disorders.

Professor Ronald Rapee, and his co-authors in their book *Helping Your Anxious Child*, highlight the many different types of anxiety as follows:

- Social Fears (eg. fears mixing with others)

- Separation Fears (eg. worried about something happening to Mum/Dad/carer)

- Generalised Worrries (eg. worries about schoolwork)

- Obsessive-Compulsive Fears (eg. has 'stuck' thinking, or 'sticky' thoughts in which something must be done repeatedly)

- Panic Fears (eg. is scared of having another panic attack)

- Post-Traumatic Fears (eg. after a traumatic incident or accident)

- Specific Fears (eg. spiders, snakes, thunderstorms)

They encourage parents to look for themes to determine the one area that causes most problems, and to focus on that theme. While all anxious children have some of these symptoms, the goal is to seek out which area is causing the greatest of difficulties for your child or young person.

Most of the strategies in this book will focus on generalised or general, anxiety or worries. Some of the above-listed anxieties may require more specialised help, particularly post-traumatic fears and obsessive-compulsive fears.

Experiencing a major trauma or incident

For children or young people experiencing major trauma, ongoing trauma, or a critical incident, professional advice is best sought immediately. Such incidents are likely to have long-term effects for children. While the steps in this program may be useful, they are unlikely to address the heart of the problem.

Is anxiety more common in children on the autism spectrum?

Yes, is the answer to this common question. Anxiety is a common feature of Autism Spectrum Disorder (ASD).

It is generally recognised amongst the clinical community that children and young people on the autism spectrum can experience crippling levels of anxiety. This impression is supported by research by Van Steensel and Heeman (2017) who found that children with

ASD had higher anxiety levels compared to typically-developing children and young people.

These results highlight the need to be vigilant about anxiety for this group of children and young people. With ASD, children and young people can be the master of disguise. They may mask their fears and anxiety so much that it cannot be detected by either family or teachers. It is common for teachers to think the student has had a good day, only to be told later about a small anxiety-provoking incident that, in the student's mind, had become the focus for the whole day.

Sometimes students on the autism spectrum articulate their anxieties slightly differently, or indeed, they may not mention them at all. If we know of the anxiety we can address it, but if we don't know about it, the individual can be suffering in silence!

More comprehensive work may be required for a child or young person to successfully manage anxieties, particularly if they are unaware that the sensations they are feeling are related to anxiety or worries. The understanding of emotions, and the regulation of emotions is particularly important work for children and young people in the ASD community.

SUMMARY OF STEP ONE

- Anxiety is a very common feeling for children and young people

- It only becomes a problem when it interferes with everyday life

- Recent research suggests that 7% of children in Australia experience anxiety disorders, and 25% of children and young people in the US experience significant anxiety at some time in their life

- Telling a child or young person to tough it out is not helpful, especially if they are struggling

- Building life-long skills to manage anxiety helps your child to cope with changes and challenges in their life

- Try not to let your own worries build anxiety in your child

- If your child has experienced a traumatic incident, try to get professional help immediately

STEP TWO

Understanding the physical effects of anxiety

UNDERSTANDING THE PHYSICAL EFFECTS OF ANXIETY

It is important for children, and adults alike, to understand the physical effects of anxiety. The physical symptoms are often indistinguishable from a 'real' illness. For instance, thoughts of: *I must be having a heart attack* often come with a fast heart rate and, *I must have food poisoning* often accompanies a feeling of nausea or vomiting.

Sometimes children take some persuading that these physical symptoms can even be symptoms of anxiety. It feels like I am sick, so I must be sick, is their thinking! The idea that these physical feelings could be coming from their thoughts seems even more impossible.

It is important to highlight here that sometimes children do have a medical reason for stomach pains or vomiting. It is always important to rule out sickness before addressing what appear to be anxiety symptoms.

There are many children's picture books that highlight feelings of anxiety. Just a few include:

- *Owl Babies* for younger children (in which little owls wait for their mother to come) by Martin Waddell
- *Your Feelings: I'm Worried* (describing feelings of anxiety for younger children) by Brian Moses
- *The Huge Bag of Worries* (in which the bag keeps growing bigger for a school girl) by Virginia Ironside

- *Worries are like Clouds* (describing how worries can be like the weather, some days are great and some are not) by Shona Innes

In her cartoon-style books for adults, Bev Aisbett lists a whole range of symptoms of anxiety.

These include:

- **Feeling sick or feeling like vomiting**
- **Having butterflies in the tummy**
- **Heart beating fast or pounding**
- **Feelings of breathing differently**
- **Having trouble thinking or making a decision**
- **Legs trembling or shaking**
- **Hands trembling or shaking**
- **Feeling dizzy**
- **Feeling jittery or nervous**
- **Sweating**
- **Looking pale or white**

Your child may experience these and other symptoms too, such as needing to go to the toilet. Encourage them to work out what they experience when feeling anxious. Children can differ greatly. Sometimes one symptom is felt intensely, sometimes there are lots of symptoms.

And sometimes a child hasn't noticed any symptoms at all, but they are very clear to everyone else!

I'm Scared

There was nothing about soccer that Antonio didn't know, well almost. He could name all the World Cup winners over the past 20 years and name the venues for each.

Every day he would practise his skills, heading the ball, bouncing the ball on his left foot, bouncing the ball on his right, and of course, shooting for goal. He could attack and defend, and in the Under 10s was asked to play in all positions.

Antonio was the star of the team but was terrified of being given the position of goalkeeper. His legs felt like lead when others were lining up to take a shot. His hands trembled, and he felt sick to the stomach. There was no way he could play this role.

He called to the coach and told him he needed to go home as he was sick. The coach was sure Antonio was not sick – he looked fine when he arrived, making jokes and laughing with his team. He had just kicked a magnificent pass to his team-mate.

The coach suggested Antonio sit on the bench and wait for a while to see if he recovered. He didn't. At the end of the match, the coach had a chat with Antonio, and advised him to see him after school the following day.

The next day, Antonio and his father met with the coach and together they watched YouTube clips of every failure great players had made. There were own goals, bad *passes and even times when players tripped over the ball. The coach highlighted to Antonio that every player makes mistakes, and every goalkeeper has balls that get past them.*

He advised Antonio to come up with a mantra like, "Even Messi, messes up!" or "No one stops all the goals!" to help remind him that he was not expected to be perfect.

And finally, the coach reminded him that Michael Jordan, famous retired basketball player had missed more than 9000 shots and lost 300 games, but reportedly said, "I've failed over and over and over again in my life. And that is why I succeed."

Antonio went home happy, knowing that it was okay to fail in his role as goalkeeper. But it still wasn't his favourite position!

I'm Scared

WHAT TO SAY

The writer of the book says that we can have some or all of these feelings when we are worried. *(See list)*

Let's look at the picture and see what you feel.
(Look at picture.)

How would you be feeling if you had a huge worry?
(Check off the feelings.)

I think you might feel... *(make a suggestion)*

I have noticed you look like you are...
(make a suggestion)

FEELING SICK OR FEELING LIKE VOMITING	HAVING TROUBLE THINKING OR MAKING A DECISION	FEELING DIZZY
HAVING BUTTERFLIES IN THE TUMMY	LEGS TREMBLING OR SHAKING	FEELING JITTERY OR NERVOUS
HEART BEATING FAST OR POUNDING	HANDS TREMBLING OR SHAKING	LOOKING PALE OR WHITE
FEELINGS OF BREATHING DIFFERENTLY	SWEATING	NEEDING TO GO TO THE TOILET

Step Two: Understanding the physical effects of anxiety

Blood to the legs

If a lion were to walk into the room, what would we do? Hopefully we would run to escape.

But, even before thinking about the lion in the room our bodies would have automatically switched on the fight/flight/freeze response. This response has been well documented around the world by scientists, physiologists, and biologists.

It is particularly important for an anxious child to understand the flight response. The fight and freeze responses can be discussed at a later stage.

Put simply, the body says: **"Blood to the legs! Blood to the legs! Run, run, run!"**

The whole body starts to scream... blood to the legs... run! This can help to explain to a child his or her physical symptoms. Go through the physical symptoms again and explain them as shown below.

Step Two: Understanding the physical effects of anxiety

WHAT TO SAY

What would happen if a lion were to walk into this room?
(Use an event that is NOT going to happen so your child doesn't think this is another thing to worry about!)

Look at the picture and draw your child's attention to the physical symptoms they often show or feel.

Your body is saying:

Blood to the legs! Blood to the legs! Run! Run! Run!

That's why you feel....

Sick, because the stomach has stopped digesting food, and processing everything. Instead it is saying: "Blood to the legs!"

The heart is beating fast because it is saying: "Blood to the legs! Get ready to run! And run fast!"

The breathing is different because it is getting ready to help with breathing fast when running.

It is hard to think because the brain is saying: "Don't do any thinking! Just run from the lion!"

I'm Scared

> *The arms and legs are shaking because they are getting ready to run fast. "Run, run, run!"*
>
> *The body feels jittery or nervous because every muscle is getting ready to "Run, run, run!"*
>
> *The head is feeling dizzy or faint because the blood is going to the legs and not the head. "Run, run, run!"*
>
> *The body is feeling sweaty because it is getting ready to cool down when the body is hot from running.*
>
> *The face or skin is pale because the blood is going to the legs, rather than the face.*

As previously stated, encourage your child to work out what symptoms they experience. Children differ greatly. Sometimes one symptom is felt intensely, sometimes there are lots of symptoms.

It is very important for your child to understand this is an automatic process. It happens without thinking, and in response to scary things, just like seeing a lion.

Step Two: Understanding the physical effects of anxiety

By understanding the process, it helps children to understand what is happening to their body. Rather than thinking: *I suddenly get an attack of random things, like stomach aches*, they can think: *There is a reason* for this feeling!

Unfortunately, this system can be turned on with other scary things too, like a math test. And you can't run away from that! Or you can, but there will be big trouble!

> *Elijah was loving his first year of school. The only trouble was that every Wednesday he would get very nauseous and sent home. It took several weeks before his teacher and foster-mother realised this happened each week.*
>
> *After some 'wondering' about this with Elijah, his foster-mother discovered it was only on days he had art classes that he got sick. Some additional supports were given to Elijah in art class, and the illness 'magically' went away. By discussing his symptoms, his foster-mother explained that Elijah had been experiencing anxiety or worries.*
>
> *Things got much better once they had talked about it, and some minor class changes made.*

It is very hard for children to notice the feelings of anxiety when they are in the throes of it, particularly if it is overwhelming. Sometimes children will notice what they are feeling, sometimes they will not. If they are feeling sick, they must be sick. If they are feeling shaky, there must be something wrong with their body. They often do not make the connection between their thoughts, such as 'school is on tomorrow', and the feeling of nausea.

It is hard for children to understand there is a connection between what they are thinking and what they are feeling. It is often important for parents or carers to wonder with their child about when the feelings occur and at what times. This can help to draw the link between the thoughts and feelings.

For instance, by saying, "I notice every Monday you get stomach pains, have you noticed that?" Or, "I wonder if feeling sick is connected to the test tomorrow?" you may be able to highlight what is happening.

> **WHAT TO SAY**
>
> Sometimes it's hard for kids to notice when they are feeling worried.
>
> Sometimes they don't realise their headaches, or tummy-aches are caused by worries.
>
> Do you think you might have some worries?
>
> Do you think your... *(physical symptoms)* ... might be a sign of some worries?
>
> There might be some way we can fix them.

> *Jacinta was very scared of clowns. She kept looking for them everywhere. Every shop she entered, she scanned for clowns. Every time she went outside she was searching for clowns.*
>
> *As the anxiety took hold she would start to quake and tremble. Her mind was scanning everywhere for threats. The little girl was terrified. She was 'under attack'.*
>
> *As her foster-parents helped her with the anxiety, she started to recognise the earliest sign of anxiety, and with other tools started to calm her mind.*

First, your child needs to understand what is happening in his or her body. Next, your child needs to know that not all anxiety is the same.

Scaling the fear, or the Worry-o-meter

Various authors, including Rapee et al, the Cool Kids programs from Macquarie University and Tony Attwood using the CAT kit, have all introduced the concept of using a scale to measure the level of fear.

Catastrophe scales, and other scales of fear are readily available online, but in essence, a scale is just like a thermometer, measuring degrees of worry.

Most people know the feeling of sheer panic when something overwhelming happens. But it is sometimes harder — for children and adults alike — to scale the anxiety on a 1-10 basis.

Creating a 1-10 scale

Usually the end points of a 1-10 scale are quite clear to the child. What makes me feel overwhelming panicky? What makes me feel calm and comfortable? They may be able to answer these questions, but cannot identify the in-between parts.

To help understand the concept of a scale it can be helpful to draw a picture of a mercury thermometer.

Talk about how it goes up and down with the temperature. On a hot day, it zooms upward, while on a cold day it plunges downward. On a warm day, it stays somewhere in-between.

If your child cannot count to ten, make a thermometer that goes up to five. If your child is fascinated by numbers they may prefer to make a thermometer that goes up to one hundred or beyond.

By looking at temperature this way, you can chat about how there are stages or scales of variation between the different temperatures.

Step Two: Understanding the physical effects of anxiety

WHAT TO SAY

Today is a hot/cold/warm day. Let's look at a picture of a thermometer and see if we can guess what the temperature is today. *(If possible, compare your guess with the actual results.)*

(When you see the temperature comment on whether your guess matched the real thing. You may say something like… Yes, nearly got it!)

Sometimes we get it right and sometimes we just get close, but usually we know the difference between a hot day and a cold day.

(It is important for your child to understand there is no absolute right number when guessing about feelings.)

We just guess at what we 'think' it is.

I'm Scared

It is important for children to understand that emotions work in the same way as temperature. Sometimes they can be high or big, and sometimes they can be low or small.

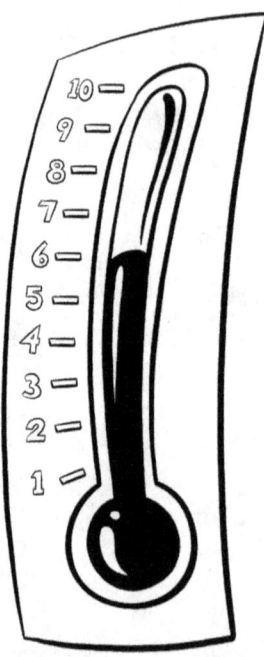

The next step is to explain that worries can go up and down, just like temperature, and just like happiness. Sometimes the worry can be very big, and sometimes it can be very small. If you are feeling your child understands these differences, it may be tempting to skip this phase. Don't!

This phase will be important to enable you and your child to have a 'secret code' in which the size of the worries can be shared.

If your child considers anxiety to be like an on-off switch, you will need to do a little more work, explaining that not all anxieties are the same. It may be worth giving extreme examples to highlight the difference. For instance, the difference between worrying if it will rain tomorrow is very different from worrying about a vicious dragon in the room.

Play another game in which you contrast many different scenarios only using your child's worries, so they can learn not all worries are the same. Remember you do not want to add extra worries for your child!

If your child still cannot understand the differences between the different levels of anxiety, you may need to skip this part.

> **WHAT TO SAY**
>
> Sometimes it might feel like all worries are the same, but feelings come in different amounts, just like temperature.
>
> Some days I am happy when it is a sunny day. Often I feel more happy if you have made me a special birthday dinner, or we go out to the movies.

I'm Scared

Let's play a game in which we think about little things that make us happy, and then something bigger that would make us more happy.

What makes you just a little bit happy?

(You may need to suggest something like a sunny day, or going for a walk)

What makes you more happy — but only a little bit more happy?

(You may need to suggest something like playing a game together)

What makes you hugely happy?

(Think of happy birthday celebrations or other times)

Step Two: Understanding the physical effects of anxiety

Mishi, a Year 6 student, loves animals. She has two cats at home, both ragdolls, and is constantly taking selfies with them. She has joined an animal welfare centre, with her parents' permission, and saves her pocket money to make a monthly donation. If a bird has fallen out of its nest she will spot it. If there are ants crossing her path, she will walk around them. She is an all-round animal protector.

One day, Mishi's parents suggested they go to the opening of a large local pet store. She loved it! There were all sorts of animals there, many of which could be petted and held.

But as the crowd began to grow, Mishi became more alarmed. She began to feel like she was being pushed and squished and feared being knocked over. The animals were great. The people were not. As she became more anxious, she remembered the anxiety scale her parents had taught her when she was younger.

"Dad, can we get out of here? This feels like an 8." Instantly, her dad responded, "Sure darling, let's move over to the side door, and if it doesn't get any better we will just leave."

As it didn't get any better, Mishi quickly left out the side door with her parents, her brother lagging behind. The crisis was averted, even if it meant taking a grumpy brother home.

The pet store is still Mishi's favourite place to be. Just without the crowds.

The Worry-o-meter

> **Activity: Making the Worry-o-meter**
> *(allow 30 minutes, depending on colouring skills)*

If you are really short of time, or feel you are artistically challenged, you can print one off from the Internet, BUT this is a very valuable activity, so try not to use the cheat or short-cut. It gives your child a chance to talk about worries in a calm space, and some valuable interaction time in which you show your respect and the importance you place on helping your child.

Often it is easiest to mark the numbers of 1-10 from the 'bulb' of the *Worry-o-meter* to the top. Occasionally, the concept of 0-100 can be introduced.

Encourage your child to colour in the numbers at the bottom — 1-3 in blue. This is not meant to be a difficult task so if your child doesn't like colouring, you should do it instead. The upper colours of 8-10 you can colour in red to emphasise this is the extreme end of the worries.

Encourage your child to choose colours for the other numbers so that the *Worry-o-meter* is meaningful for them.

Begin by asking your child to list activities when they feel calm and have *no* worries. For the highly-anxious child, there may be no activity apart from sleeping in which they feel calm. That's okay.

Step Two: Understanding the physical effects of anxiety

Start with that! After the first three activities are listed at 1-3, move up to the top of the *Worry-o-meter*.

Now, this may become a much easier task. Ask your child to think of their most fearful experience. Remember it must be an experience rather than an imagined activity. So, 'thinking of Mum and Dad dying' would be okay, 'Mum and Dad dying' is not, unless your child has actually experienced this.

Step Two: Understanding the physical effects of anxiety

Things to remember before starting this activity:

- The process of this activity is more important than how good the *Worry-o-meter* looks
- This is the child's *Worry-o-meter*, not yours!
- Your child may have more than one activity at one number. This is only a problem if there is nothing in the middle
- By the end you will have a secret code that you can use together (eg. Dad, this is a 10!)

> **WHAT TO SAY**
>
> Now we are going to make something. Let's use some paper and colouring pencils. We are going to make our very own Worry-o-meter.
>
> We are going to use this shape to make something like a thermometer with numbers from 1-10.
>
> Next, we are going to colour the different levels. This part at the bottom will be blue. Can you colour up to this line for 3? The top part will be red. Can you colour down to this line for 8?

WHAT TO SAY

Now, we need to think about what you would be doing when you never have worries. Can you think of something? *(You may need to offer a suggestion.)*

I will write that beside the number 1.

What about when you are still in the blue zone but you only have a teeny bit of worry? It's probably number 2. What would you be doing then?

(If the young person suggests several activities, determine which would be number 2 and which would be number 3. But, it is perfectly fine to have more than one activity at a number.)

Next, move up to the red zone…

Let's look at the red zone. I wonder what a 10 would be?

(If the young person doesn't have any ideas, make some suggestions.)

Step Two: Understanding the physical effects of anxiety

Let's put some other things in for numbers 8 and 9.
(Again, you may need to make some suggestions.)

What colours should we put for these numbers?
(Add colours and activities as necessary.)

Wow, you have done a great job here! Now we have a secret code we can use when you are feeling worried.

You might say to me, "No, this isn't a worry, this is a 5. Or help me, this is a 10!"

Learning to calm the body

In real-life, once we have escaped from a ferocious lion, our body calms down, and eventually life goes back to normal, with only a near-miss recalled and an exciting tale to tell.

But what happens when our body is constantly under attack from anxiety? In many instances, we need to teach the body to calm down. This is where various calming activities such as relaxation activities, belly-breathing and slow-breathing can play a part.

These strategies have been studied and expounded by Buddhists, meditation specialists, mental health professionals and others.

Dougie had heard of wildfires happening. He knew they were very dangerous, and he knew people died in them.

One day, as summer approached he looked around his yard and saw some toys lying near the house. This was bad. He knew fires could catch hold of anything near the house and knew everyone needed to keep their yards clean. Much to his carer's surprise he immediately started cleaning and sweeping the yard.

The little seven year old did not understand that wildfires did not usually attack the suburbs of the city they lived in. The forest was a long way away.

Dougie's carers knew they would have to start calming Dougie or it was going to be a very long summer. A very, very long summer!

They explained the dynamics of wildfires. They are more likely to occur on hot, windy days, with low humidity, particularly after a dry spell. But they won't occur on every summer's day.

There was no point in pretending they didn't happen. They did. There had been a fire in the nearby forest two years ago, and the family regularly stopped on the side of the road to look at the regrowth. Won't be doing that anymore, his carers thought.

His carers persuaded Dougie they knew a lot about wildfires and knew exactly what to do if the fire came

I'm Scared

> into the suburbs. They would never take risks, they argued, and the house could be built again. They suggested Dougie make a list of his most precious things, just in case they needed to leave one day. But, they pointed out, he wouldn't need to put those things aside, because probably that day would never come.
>
> In addition to teaching him some facts about wildfires they decided to teach him some breathing techniques so he could calm himself. They decided on using a meditation app on his school tablet. This would mean he could use it anytime, anywhere.
>
> Dougie's carers encouraged him to practise his breathing every night when he went to bed. Eventually, he became skilled at slowing his breathing and thinking calm thoughts.
>
> And to this day, the wildfire hasn't come.

Strategies for self-soothing

Teaching the body to calm is a mighty big challenge, especially when your heart feels like it is going to pound out of your chest. Finding something to focus on can help, but it can be hard to find just the right thing.

Many schools have introduced simple meditation and breathing classes to children and young people, and many apps have been devised to help with this process. By following these calming strategies, distractions can be reduced and even ignored. Sometimes just hearing the rhythmic sound of the breath can be soothing, sometimes just a beautiful scene can be focused on to help create a sense of calm.

Teaching calming skills is an important tool to help train the mind to relax. By relaxing, the mind is not overtaken by worrying thoughts. Self-calming is particularly useful to practise at night-time; when a child or young person is going to bed, the worries are likely to emerge.

There are many apps available on smartphones or tablets to help with these skills, such as *Smiling Mind*. This app has been well-researched and is regularly used in schools throughout Australia. Apparently, even the Australian cricket team used it — a useful commendation for budding sports stars.

But there are many other apps, too, some of which include:

- Breathing Zone
- Chakra Chime
- Smiling Mind
- MyCalmBeat
- Calm

It is important that you find one that feels comfortable for your child. So, if none of them seem appropriate keep searching. Some young people like to have a sound to listen to, some do not. Some like a beautiful scene as in *Calm*, some do not. It is important to keep exploring to see what technique will suit your child or young person.

It is important children understand that these skills need to be practised regularly, so they can 'just switch them on'. Once the child or young person has developed this skill, it can be very powerful, and can help to reduce the level of anxiety.

> *Georgie's friend had been away from school for a couple of days, and her mother suggested she visit her friend after school. "You know the way to her house," she encouraged. "Just a short visit then walk on home."*
>
> *After school, Georgie set off to Stephanie's house. As she came around the second corner, after the school crossing, she realised she had taken a wrong turn. She was immediately overwhelmed by anxiety. Panicked she wondered what to do.*
>
> *Quickly she remembered her anxiety techniques. She practised some slow breathing and found she could think more clearly. "When I stay calm, I think better," she recited, and re-traced her steps to school to start again.*
>
> *The second journey was more successful, and this time she was met at the door by Stephanie's mother with chocolate-chip cookies. By the time she got home, Georgie recounted her mistaken steps to her mother. "It worked! It worked!" she said, as she recalled her slow breathing.*

For some children, their level of stress and anxiety is so great that they cannot focus on the simple activity of breathing because their mind is racing. Sometimes another activity, such as colouring, playing music, or completing a complicated jigsaw puzzle can put them in that state of calm, but sometimes even that will not help. Sometimes an adult may just comment on what they notice about the child's breathing, or try to develop a rhythmic breathing pattern of their own.

> *Andy was a very cute, but anxious boy. He was terrified of storms, and any time he heard thunder or saw lightning, he would start to shake. He was so distressed he could not focus on the words his mother was saying, nor could he focus on his breathing. It was all too hard! The only thing he focused on was whether another clap of thunder was coming.*
>
> *He could not do other activities like puzzles or listening to music. He was simply shaking and listening. His mother was very wise. She hugged him tight and held him close and recited a mantra of, "This will be okay. This will pass", while gently rocking him.*
>
> *As Andy gradually calmed, his mother switched to focus on her own breathing and counting while still rocking. Eventually the storm passed, and Andy could return to life. It took a long while to get over the thunderstorms, but this was the beginning.*

The following technique is a very simple breathing technique to teach even very young children.

> ### WHAT TO SAY
>
> We are going to practise some slow breathing.
>
> You know when you jump into a pool and take a big breath, like this? *(Demonstrate taking a big breath.)* That is NOT what we are going to do.
>
> We are going to take little breaths, little-bit by little-bit, and count up to 4. Let's try together.
>
> I will count out loud, and we will breathe in very slowly. If you can breathe through your nose that's great. Otherwise breathing through your mouth is fine.
>
> Let's go... 1... 2... 3... 4... **Hold it** *(for one second)* **and now breathe out... 1... 2... 3... 4...**
>
> If that was a little tricky we can try blowing gently on a candle to make it flicker. That helps to slow down breathing out.
>
> Sometimes people like to practise blowing bubbles in a glass of water, too. This helps to slow the breathing out as well.

Step Two: Understanding the physical effects of anxiety

WHAT TO SAY

We need to practise this breathing business lots, because with lots of practice, it can help to 'turn off' those worry feelings.

And you know the best bit? Nobody needs to know you are practising.

If someone asks what you are doing, all you need to say is: "Just breathing, aren't you?"

SUMMARY OF STEP TWO

- Encourage your child to notice the physical symptoms he/she experiences when feeling worried or anxious

- There is a link between physical body sensations and anxiety. Essentially when worried, the body is saying "Blood to the legs, blood to the legs, run, run, run!"

- Remember, physical symptoms of anxiety occur for smaller things like school tests, just as much as when faced with a ferocious animal

- Scale the fears to understand that all worries are not equal

- Look at a thermometer to help your child understand temperature differences, and then make a Worry-o-meter as a secret code for discussion with your child

- Practise relaxation or breathing strategies regularly

STEP THREE

Linking thoughts and feelings

LINKING THOUGHTS AND FEELINGS

It is important for children to understand that thoughts are linked with feelings. Sometimes it feels like the feelings come first, then the thoughts, but a useful cartoon can help here.

Imagine this on two separate days — one, an everyday breakfast, the other the boy's birthday:

In both situations, the mother says the same thing. In both situations, the child says the same thing. The only thing that is different, is the thought process (although of course, it is the child's birthday). In the first picture the child is happy, in the second he is sad, or dismayed. This comic strip highlights how our thoughts affect our feelings.

Ronald Rapee and his co-authors describe the link between thoughts and feelings: 'certain feelings go along with certain thoughts and anxious feelings tend to go along with thoughts of danger' (p 50 *Helping Your Anxious Child*, Rapee et al., 2008)

Many children assume the feeling comes before the thought. It is much harder to access the thought, whereas the feeling 'is just there'. Therefore, they think the feeling must be driving this.

However, thoughts affect feelings, feelings affect behaviour, and behaviour often links back to the feelings in a kind of triangle.

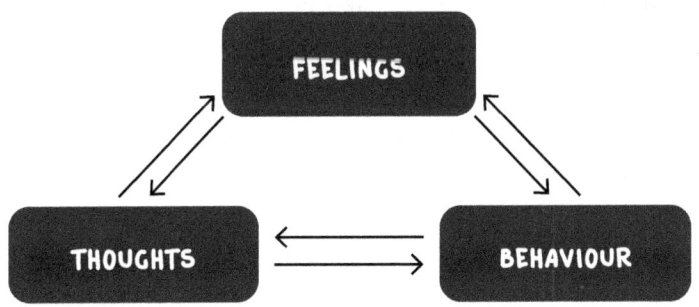

Once children understand this link, they may be able to think about the thoughts they have before the feelings.

I'm Scared

Imogen is very scared at night. She cannot go to sleep without her parents sleeping beside her. She cries and becomes intensely distressed if her parents suggest she tough it out. She insists, "It feels so scary just lying in bed!" What's more, her thoughts about bad stuff happening just keep going around and around.

By asking Imogen to talk about her thoughts, often termed 'unhelpful' thoughts, her parents begin to realise she is terrified bad people will come in the middle of the night and kidnap her. By starting to talk about these unhelpful thoughts, her parents help Imogen to think about her safety differently. They remind her they have two very large dogs, one that sleeps in her room, and they have locks on the doors and windows.

They also remind her that bad people don't like to get caught. Imagine all the commotion of four people, plus two large dogs, if someone came into their house! Imogen began to be reassured. Bad people don't like a commotion. There would be too much noise in her house, she reasoned.

This helpful thought was used to replace the unhelpful thoughts.

Step Three: Linking thoughts and feelings

Sometimes we need our thoughts to change for our feelings to change. In this situation, Imogen tried to change her thoughts, which then helped to change her feelings.

> ### WHAT TO SAY
>
> Some very clever psychologists and scientists have worked out there is a link between what we think, or say to ourselves, and how we feel.
>
> We often think the feelings come first, and then the thoughts. But it is actually the other way around. Thoughts can come at lightning speed!
>
> If we were to see a lion in the forest, our first thought is 'A lion!' Then our body does the rest, "Blood to the legs, blood to the legs, blood to the legs! Run, run, run!"
>
> The thoughts come first, and then we act.
>
> Imagine if we just went around in life, running from things, and we didn't know what we were running from. We would just run without thinking. What a funny world it would be!

Helpful thoughts and unhelpful thoughts

For children and young people, the link can be drawn between helpful thoughts and unhelpful thoughts. The unhelpful thought is what is making them feel uncomfortable, and even worse than uncomfortable. The helpful thought is one that makes them feel a little better.

Children are usually familiar with the experience of self-talk.

They will understand the experience of: "Wow, I'm great at this!" is very different from "How come everyone can do this, except me?"

Often, children and young people with worries are experts at coming up with unhelpful thoughts. Adults can be experts at unhelpful thoughts too!

> ## WHAT TO SAY
>
> **We have lots of thoughts in our heads. Sometimes we have helpful thoughts. Sometimes we have unhelpful thoughts.**
>
> **A helpful thought might be:**
>
> *I'm great at this!*
> *Yeah, I've got this!*
> *Wow, I can do this!*
>
> **Remember when...** *(mention a success your child has had)*, **I think you might have had some helpful thoughts then.**
>
> **But sometimes we are really good at coming up with unhelpful thoughts, especially if we have worries.**
>
> **Unhelpful thoughts are like:**
>
> *I can't do this!*
> *I'm never going to learn this.*
> *We are all going to die!*

Remember the story of the Chicken Licken or Henny Penny, who thought the sky was falling in and predicted disaster everywhere? Apparently, this story goes back centuries. Perhaps this story depicts the first incidence of an anxiety disorder!

Statements like "We are all going to die!" and "The sky is falling in", as was said by Chicken Licken, are unhelpful thoughts. Unhelpful thoughts don't need to be so extreme, but generally have a tone of danger, and a sense of feeling unsafe.

Helpful thoughts

I am the best in the class at this would be a helpful thought. By now, you know the anxious person is not so good at coming up with helpful thoughts but is usually excellent at coming up with negative thoughts.

For children who are experts in worrying, it is like they are wired to find problems and worries. I sometimes liken it to the intense concentration of searching for a lost pet. They are focused on only one thing and nothing else matters. They are looking and searching for it everywhere.

The focus on the negative thought can be intense for an anxious child.

It is important for children and young people to know that you take their concerns seriously. That is why it is not helpful to tell them, "Don't worry about that!" It is better to critically analyse the chances of something happening. Of course, if you can bias the statistics in any way, to help reduce the likelihood of it happening, so much the better!

For instance, you may want to give burglary rates for the whole state, rather than your region or vice versa.

Many concerns for children and young people centre around their own safety and/or the safety of their caregivers. It seems to take around 5-7 years before the child realises 'Where's the guarantee that you will be with me forever?' and 'Where's the guarantee that I will be safe?' Once they have had this thought, it is hard to get rid of. Where *is* the guarantee?

And, once they have had this thought, it cannot be brushed off lightly. They may know of another student at school whose parent has died. They may know someone who has been in a car accident. And they may be all too familiar with the sensationalist news items suggesting we are all going to die from an overdose of sugar, or outbreaks of violence.

Step Three: Linking thoughts and feelings

WHAT TO SAY

We can have helpful thoughts and unhelpful thoughts. Helpful thoughts would be like:
I'm great at this! **and** *Wow, that was easy!*

Unhelpful thoughts would be like:
Why did I say that? I am a loser!
or *Whoa, that dog is going to bite me!*

Let's see if we can think of some more helpful thoughts and unhelpful thoughts. *(If this is too hard, suggest some helpful thoughts for the child.)*

(Your child is probably very good at coming up with unhelpful thoughts, even if they can't come up with any now.)

DON'T *suggest any unhelpful thoughts, as we don't want to add to his/her own list of unhelpful thoughts*

Respecting the worries

Now, finally, it is time to address the worries your child is experiencing. This will be a very hard thing for them to do. Respect that.

Choose a time and place that is calm and relaxed for the child, in which they can talk about these issues. Ask them to think of all their worries. You will need to make a list, and it may be a very long list. Do not make comments about the worries but keep asking if there are any more.

Remember, this task should be done with great respect.

As a 7 year old, I visited New York City, and spent way too much time worrying a jaguar would leap through the 5th floor window of our hotel, because my nature book said jaguars lived in North America. Nothing your child or young person says is stupid or silly. Everything is valid. They have probably come to a very logical conclusion. It is just they are using the wrong facts.

Mitchy was terrified of injections. The whole idea of going to the doctor was scary enough, let alone the idea that he would need to have an injection. Last time, he had a shot, when he was five years old, his head went woozy and he felt sick and dizzy. He was NEVER going through that again!

This is what his mother faced after the doctor had recommended he have a flu injection, so he did not infect his brother who had low immunity. Mitchy knew the flu could seriously affect his brother, and yet the whole idea of the injection was too much for him.

His mother pleaded with him, begged him, and offered various rewards, all to no avail. She became very angry and demanded that he have the shot, but Mitchy remained insistent that he was NOT having the shot.

Finally, Mitchy's Mum accepted it was too much to ask of him. He was terrified of the whole idea. His mother told him she respected how anxious he was becoming. But, several weeks later Mitchy came to her, and suggested perhaps he could have the shot if the doctor came to their home, rather than having it at the doctor's surgery. And then, he proposed, he could play a brand-new X-Box game as soon as he had the shot.

As Mitchy's brother had a life-threatening illness, his mother had no hesitation in accepting this offer. The doctor was also willing to oblige. The plan went like clockwork. Mitchy barely noticed the injection as he pressed 'play' for the new game.

I'm Scared

By respecting Mitchy's high anxiety, his mother gave him an opportunity to calm down and think of other suggestions, and of course it included a new game!

Finding the facts

Confronting the facts is very difficult for adults and young people alike. What is the likelihood of dying young? What is the likelihood of being the target of a random kidnapping?

When stories in the media abound, it is hard to consider that this is un-likely. For children and young people, it seems probable. Especially as they cannot conceive that other factors need to be considered.

So when thinking about the likelihood of dying in a car accident there are things to think about, such as how safe is the driver? How much experience do they have on the roads? Do they drive for 12 hours straight without a break? Do they drive around at 2am?

For the young person, it is important to consider that all these factors play a part in determining the likelihood of an accident. Not just whether they are driving on the road or not. A child or young person considers we all have an equal likelihood of dying. Children and young people may assume all factors are equal; they are not, and they need to understand this.

It is also possible to explain the odds in a positive way. If the driver has no speeding tickets, bonus points. If the driver does not drive through red lights, bonus points. If the driver is tucked up in bed, rather than driving for 12 hours straight, bonus points.

Step Three: Linking thoughts and feelings

Suddenly the world does not seem like a such a bad place. The world is a place where our behaviour sometimes dictates the risks in life. If we love to jump off buildings without a parachute, we may not live as long as someone who chooses to stay on the ground.

Sometimes, some blunt examples are necessary. Give the example of crossing the road without looking to see whether cars are coming. Just walk across and take your chances. Good idea? Probably not.

I once heard the statistic that the most dangerous time of life is in the first twelve months. Babies are not aware of so many things. The dangers of electricity, heat, ingesting small items such as batteries and the weather outdoors, are just a few. Just ask a new mother — exhausting!

This is a useful statistic, although I cannot find its source. For children have all lived through the first twelve months. They feel successful. They are already survivors.

However, a note of caution, you may not want to mention this to the child who has a baby sibling, or is likely to have a newborn sibling, as it would just be another source of worry.

The following process will help to draw the child or young person's attention to needing evidence for their fear. If they are fearful of a kidnapping, it may be important to highlight that there have been no kidnappings in the area for the past 15 years. Remember anything longer than 15 years ago is likely to be 'the olden days' for your child or young person.

On the other hand, if there have been kidnappings, your child will need to understand what steps you are taking to keep them safe. We all take steps to keep safe each day. We look before we cross the road, we lock the door as we go out, we keep a look out for people behaving in unusual ways, we obey the speed limit.

It will be important to highlight these steps to your child or young person. Locked doors, locked windows, dogs, security lights all keep 'bad' people away. Also, you may wish to highlight that usually 'bad people' don't like to be caught, so anything that helps them be captured will be a deterrent. Bad people don't want you to call the police. Bad people don't want to be seen. These are our helpful thoughts.

> **WHAT TO SAY**
>
> Okay, so now we need to work out how likely the fears and worries are.
>
> We need to make a table of the worries, on paper or on the computer, to work out how likely the fears and worries are.

Step Three: Linking thoughts and feelings

Important points to consider during this conversation:

- Even though you want to minimise the risks, you still need to be honest with the fears and worries

- Choose an example to start with that will be easy to work through, and one that is not likely to occur

- Look for evidence openly and honestly

WHAT TO SAY

In the table, we will put 3 columns:

The Worry	The Evidence?	How likely?

Let's see what evidence there is for these worries. Let's do...

Now, let's think about how likely it is. Do we need to search the Internet, or the newspapers? Who should we call to find how often this happens?

Now, we need to work out how likely it is to happen to us. We need to think about what might protect us from that happening? For instance, we lock the house when we go out.

Step Three: Linking thoughts and feelings

SOME QUESTIONS TO ASK COULD BE

Would I let you hang out with bad people?

Do we have protection with locks?

Do we walk out of the house leaving it all unlocked?

Do I drive safely?

Do we have a dog who makes some noise?

Now, we need to work out if each scary thing is...

Very likely/likely/unlikely/or very unlikely.

What do you think?

I'm Scared

Janie was scared she would be kidnapped at night. Each night she went to bed thinking tonight was the night she would be kidnapped. She had heard stories of people being kidnapped, and had even seen a tv show about it. Every time she heard a noise, she suspected it was kidnappers prowling around. She often did not get to sleep till midnight, and would often wake through the night when she heard a noise and run to her parents' bed.

Her mother, with help from a psychologist, completed the above exercise with Janie. Janie did not know of any kidnappings in her home town, and when they checked the Internet, found there had been none. There had been one time in the past five years when someone tried to encourage a girl into a car with him. The girl had run away.

It seemed it was very unlikely bad people would kidnap Janie at night, especially as they had a yappy dog who would make lots of noise. Her mother reminded Janie of the importance of stranger danger, to not take rides with strangers, and to run away if someone was behaving suspiciously.

Janie slept better from that point, but still regularly sought reassurance from her mother about people who might try to offer her rides.

There are dangers out there

Unfortunately, there are dangers in the world. We do need to keep our children and young people safe, and we need to teach them how to stay safe.

It is unrealistic to say there are no dangers in the world because everyone knows there are dangers in the world. We need to explain what to do, think realistically, and have plans for when bad things happen. It is much better to teach a child what to do if the house catches fire, rather than say "Don't worry. It won't happen!"

Remember, sometimes fear is designed to keep us safe.

> William was nine years old when he visited Christchurch, New Zealand and witnessed the devastation created by the 2011 earthquake. So many buildings had been destroyed, even though it was 12 months after the event and the story of the Canterbury Television (CTV) Building collapsing and catching fire troubled him greatly.
>
> When he returned home to Australia, he was completely preoccupied with thoughts of the earthquake. It had been unexpected. Many people were killed, and thousands injured. What happened if it occurred at his house? Was he safe catching public transport? He knew some people died when part of a building fell on a bus.

> *He could not get to sleep at night worrying that an earthquake may occur at any time. His family could all be killed!*
>
> *As his father watched William's anxiety increase he decided to help William with some facts and evidence. Australia is not prone to earthquakes like New Zealand, he pointed out. And, indeed, when they looked at a map of areas likely to be hit by earthquakes, they lived in one of the safest parts of Australia.*

But what if you don't live in one of the safest parts? What if, unlike William, there is indeed a reason to worry? There is still a need to collect facts, although you may not want to use all of them. It is not helpful to say "Yes, we live in the most dangerous part of the world. And we are all going to die!"

It is important to explain some actions if there is a chance of some danger happening. It is unlikely to be a frequent, ongoing threat. Otherwise why would that town or regional area be settled in the first place. The San Francisco Bay region is a clear case in point. Would all those very clever people live in Silicon Valley if they thought an earthquake was imminent?

But, at the same time, it is important to establish what action to take if an earthquake occurred. While it is not necessary to explain this protocol to William living in Australia, if William were living in New Zealand this information may be vital to help him stay calm. He would need to understand there is a way to stay safe in case this happens, and here is a plan so we know what to do.

Using mantras

Saying a helpful thought over and over can be like a mantra. If your child or young person can recite it over and over, it can be soothing. It also means the helpful thought can be accessed more easily once it has been practised over and again. Choose one that works for you.

Some helpful mantras could be…

At school, when work is hard

- When I stay calm, I think better (Tony Attwood)
- Try, try, try again (attributed to Thomas H. Palmer)
- Mistakes happen on the way to learning (Carol Gray)
- I just can't do it, yet (Carol Dweck)
- I've done it before, I can do it again (Tony Attwood)

For fear of dangerous events

- Worries are just my body's way of saying 'stay safe'
- I've done it before, I can do it again (Tony Attwood)
- When I stay calm, I think better (Tony Attwood)
- Brave and strong. Brave and strong!
- I know what to do in an emergency
- I know this (event) is unlikely
- Noises happen every night in every house. Sometimes we hear them, sometimes we don't

For tests

- It may not be fun, but it has to be done (Carol Gray)
- Tests show how good a teacher is, not just the student
- I can only do the best I can

When friends are being mean

- Friendship includes forgiveness
- Sometimes life isn't fair
- Sometimes we just have to get over it, and move on
- Friends aren't friends if they treat you badly all the time

Once you have found a useful mantra, keep using it to help manage the worries.

SUMMARY OF STEP THREE

- Treat every fear with respect. It may seem unlikely to you, but it seems likely to your child or young person

- Our thoughts and feelings are linked

- Our self-talk can affect how we are feeling

- We all have helpful thoughts and unhelpful thoughts

- Look for the evidence honestly and openly. How likely is it that my worst fear will happen?

- Make a table for the evidence to determine the likelihood of events

- Use mantras to help create helpful thoughts

I'm Scared

STEP FOUR

Pushing through

PUSHING THROUGH

Sometimes the process of conquering fear seems immense. The mountain to climb seems overwhelming. Just like climbing Mt Everest, the preparation has been done, but still there is more to do. It's exhausting, and it is around this point that everyone is ready to give up.

The Intrepid anxiety warrior

It is important to remember 'hitting the wall' is a common experience for intrepid anxiety warriors and marathon runners alike. I always marvelled at the way some marathon runners quit during the Olympics. They ran for many kilometres or miles then 'hit the wall' and gave up. And I think, *Surely you have run this distance before you came to the Olympics? Surely you knew how far you needed to run? Surely you have done it before… and can do it again?*

It may be easy to get started on the journey of battling anxiety, but it is also tempting to give up when it gets difficult. If you think you are not making much progress, you may be feeling like that runner.

Climbing the mountain of fear is just as difficult and just as tempting to give up as the marathon. After scaling the fear, and working out how likely the events are, the next step is to push through.

Step Four: Pushing through

Sometimes it can be helpful to draw a picture of a series of stairs to represent the challenges ahead. For a child, looking to the top of the stairs or success, the whole thing can seem insurmountable. But if you are asking them to just complete the first step, that may be possible.

Antonia was scared of sleeping over at her friend's house. It was just too hard. Her friend had slept many times over at Antonia's house, but Antonia could not sleep anywhere else.

She had tried to sleep at her grandparent's house but needed to come home at midnight. She had tried to sleep at her cousin's house, but that was too hard as well. It all seemed hopeless!

Antonia's mother prepared a series of steps (or stairs) for her, in which the top stair was sleeping over at her friend's house. But there were 10 stairs in-between. What a lot of stairs!

The first stair, her Mum explained, was to visit her friend's house during the day. Easy! She had already done that many times. And she did.

The next stair was just a little harder. She had to pack her bag for a sleepover-even though it wasn't happening, and go to her cousin's house. Her mother had explained to her aunt what was happening, and all went well.

The next stair was for her to take her bag and take out all her things for the pretend sleepover. And so, the stairs went on. Relatively easy and achievable tasks for each step of the way.

Then, the tasks became a little harder. She had to get ready to sleep at her cousin's house, even though she was getting up and leaving before sleeping. This she did several times over.

Now, things were getting tougher. On this stair, she had to lie in bed for 30 minutes in her cousin's room before her mother collected her. If she fell asleep, she would still be woken up to go home

Antonia was loving these tasks. She got to spend lots of time with her cousin, who she adored, and the mums were enjoying getting together too. But at the 6th stair, things came crashing down.

Antonia had been managing all the stairs so well, her Mum set her a new task of sleeping over at her cousin's. All went well, she went to bed, and went to sleep until 1am, when she woke up. Crying uncontrollably, she went to her aunt's room and asked to go home. What a disaster!

Her Mum explained this was not a disaster. In fact, this was expected. At some point, it was expected the task would be too great, and they would just go back to the lower stair (and not the beginning).

And so, the tasks continued. Gradually growing more complicated and more difficult, but always with the understanding that her mother and aunt would arrange for Antonia to go home, no matter the time.

Antonia went home at 1am, at 2.30am, at 4.00am and frustratingly once at 5.30am, when she had nearly

> made it through the night. But eventually, and I do mean eventually, this intrepid anxiety warrior made it through to the other side. She slept all night long at her cousin's house. This started to become a weekly event until Antonia managed to start the same challenges at her friend's house.
>
> Now, she can manage all sleepover requests with only a little anxiety.
>
> **(see Appendix 3 for the design of these stairs.)**

It is important to remember that an anxious child is always likely to be anxious. A long-term study has suggested that temperament tends to be consistent across ages. That's why it is important to start developing skills that can help across a lifetime.

The Australian Temperament Project (ATP) – is a long-term study that followed, and continues to follow, a large group of Victorians from their birth to age 30 years.

'The ATP is a joint project between the Australian Institute of Family Studies, the Royal Children's Hospital, the University of Melbourne and Deakin University, and is one of only a few in the world with information on three generations of study members — the young people, their parents, and now the young people's own children.'

Since temperament tends to be consistent across ages, the aim should not be to 'cure' the anxiety. It is to make the anxiety manageable throughout life.

> **WHAT TO SAY**
>
> Now, we get to one of the harder parts for both of us.
>
> This is the part where we both have to push through.
>
> I am not allowed to get cross and frustrated and give up on you, and neither are you allowed to give up on yourself. Giving up is not an option.
>
> Let's watch a YouTube clip of a 5,000m runner at the Summer Olympics at Rio in 2016. It's called the Most Beautiful Moment of Rio 2016 and can be found on YouTube.
>
> We are going to be like the injured runner. Not giving up. We are in this together. We are going to get to the end.

I'm Scared

WHAT TO SAY

It is like we are going to climb a mountain with a whole lot of steps or stairs. Let's think of a time when we had to climb a whole lot of stairs to get somewhere. Can you think of anything? Did we get tired along the way? Was it a relief to get to the top?

You know when you have to climb a whole lot of stairs, and when you are at the bottom it looks like you have so far to go? Then when you get half-way, it doesn't look so bad, and then finally when you get nearly to the top, it all seems possible?

That's kind of like the stairs we are going to do here. We are going to make some stairs for something that seems impossible to do.

Give your child an example of a goal that seems possible to achieve. Don't make the first example too hard because we want everyone to achieve success!

For some children, they can aim for a fear at a number 10 on the *Worry-o-meter*. For others, it is best to aim for a number 8, achieve success, and then go back to tackle the number 10. You are the expert on your child. Think carefully about which task will be the best choice.

Now, use the template in the back of the book to build your stairs.

> ## WHAT TO SAY
>
> Now we have to work out what stairs to use.
>
> You get to stand on the first stair with something you can already do. Let's put some stickers there. Yay, we are on our way!
>
> The last stair is something that you can't get to at the moment, but you would like to be able to do.
>
> And now we have to make up the stairs in-between. Think of what tasks are just a little harder than the previous one, or think of tasks that are a little easier than the top one.

Important note:

- **There is no set number of stairs that suits all occasions. Stairs need to gradually make a task harder and to be designed to suit your child's ability**
- **Most stairs should have a task**
- **If you are struggling to make up the stairs in-between look at the example in the back of the book. It is okay if one or two stairs don't have tasks. You will probably think of something, when you come to it**

The importance of the accelerator and the clutch

We have been talking about climbing a mountain. So, why am I now introducing accelerators and clutches?

I would ask you to indulge me for just a moment in a mixed metaphor. I have pondered over how to describe this with the mountain analogy but can't think of an appropriate metaphor. Also, I find that many of my clients understand this concept when we talk about cars using an accelerator and clutch. So, if you will forgive the change of gear, and the poor pun, here we go.

When driving a manual, or stick-shift car, one of the greatest challenges is to coordinate the use of the accelerator and clutch when changing gear. If you use too much accelerator, you will hear the engine revving like crazy, and if you use too much clutch you will stall and come to a sudden stop. The whole art of driving a manual car is to get the balance just right for a smooth ride.

It is the same with anxiety. Too much accelerator, or pushing hard on the anxiety, means that we have failed, and we are going straight back to the beginning. Too much clutch, we are not moving forward. Balance is the key. We want to use just enough pressure, but not too much.

If you have an automatic car, you may want to seek out a friend or family-member who can show you a manual car, or who can even demonstrate what happens when the car stalls.

> **WHAT TO SAY**
>
> When we are working on these worries we need to think about how hard to push.
>
> It seems it is a bit like driving a car. Have you noticed when we drive we use different foot pedals? One pedal makes the car goes faster, one pedal makes the car stop, and in some cars, there is another pedal to help change gears.
>
> In cars like that we need to carefully balance the two pedals: the accelerator and the clutch. If we don't get a good balance we can bunny-hop down the street, or just suddenly stop, which is not fun.

Step Four: Pushing through

> So, with our work we need to think about getting the balance right. Not too much, not too little.
>
> If we push too hard, we might end up going back to the start again. Not fun!
>
> If we push too little, we won't go anywhere, and then life will just stay the same. So, we need to get the balance just right.
>
> Do you think we can do this? I think we can.

We all are driven by rewards

Most people wouldn't turn up at work if they weren't paid. Most people wouldn't do the most difficult of tasks if there wasn't some reward in it for them. For some, the reward is the feeling of success, for others it is more tangible, like the pay cheque at the end of the week. We all need rewards.

Your child or young person may feel that they are putting themselves through a nightmare. Why shouldn't there be some reward?

And yes, there should be. Don't be afraid of other terms like bribery and corruption. This is not what we are talking about. Everyone needs the encouragement of a reward to get through really hard times. And these are really hard times! Never underestimate just how hard this is for your child or young person. Remember, it may be the hardest thing they ever have to do.

Consider whether small rewards are appropriate for each stair along the way, or whether you decorate the chart of steps with colourful stickers for each step of the way. Some children, especially younger ones, will enjoy putting beautiful stickers of the latest movie on their chart. Other children will be more mercenary. "What's in it for me?" they may ask. But usually the joy of getting closer to the goal of something they can't yet do, will be reward enough.

The rewards can be an important part of the process, particularly if you discuss appropriate rewards. Often children or young people are surprisingly humble in their choice of rewards. But, if your child is planning on "a... new car!" as their reward, you may need to discuss appropriate rewards for appropriate tasks!

> *Ned, a typical six year old, was terrified of dogs. It didn't matter whether they were big or small. Whenever he saw a dog he would start to shake. If dogs appeared on television, he would turn it off.*
>
> *His parents were concerned by the extreme nature of these responses. Ned had a fright when, at the age of four, a dog unexpectedly jumped on him. But at the*

time he seemed to have recovered. However, his fears gradually became greater and greater.

His parents created a series of stairs for Ned that started with looking at a picture of a dog in a magazine for ten seconds. This was usually the time it took for Ned to notice the picture, so was something he could already do.

His parents then put together some other very small steps for Ned to try. They gradually increased looking at the picture from ten seconds to thirty seconds, using pictures of very cute, fluffy dogs. Each time Ned tolerated seeing the picture he would get some racing car stickers, his current passion.

Once Ned had tolerated looking at the pictures of cute dogs, his parents encouraged him to watch YouTube clips of dogs doing funny antics. Ned loved these clips, and sometimes needed to be reminded to choose a sticker.

Gradually his parents encouraged Ned to watch dogs from afar to see if they might do anything funny. Usually they didn't, but Ned seemed satisfied to watch.

Finally, Ned was introduced to a friend's dog who was calm and predictable in nature. Ned patted the dog and talked to it for a short time.

Ned continues to enjoy watching funny animal YouTube clips, but does not wish to have a dog in the family. That's okay. He can tolerate dogs nearby when necessary.

Parenting styles

One of the crucial parts to this journey is to recognise your own parenting style. There is no judgement here. If you are an anxious parent, you are likely to be passing on that anxiety to your children, sometimes without noticing it.

It is important to understand that there is no prejudice here about the way you parent. But, you must be aware of how you parent. The more collaborative you are, the more your child or young person, will feel like you are working together.

If you are pointing out all the dangers in the world, the world becomes a mighty scary place! It can be a good idea to keep discussion of world events to a minimum. Only share as much information as your child can process at this stage of his or her emotional development. Recognise that at a young age your child may not be able to cope with the thought of a world war breaking out.

If you have a more authoritarian style you may be telling your child or young person they will achieve success with these stairs without recognising the amount of support that is needed. You may feel that you, as the parent or carer, have got this sorted out and that they should just follow this pathway and all will be fine! But it doesn't work like that.

The child or young person needs to feel you are travelling with them on this journey. They need you to understand how hard it is for them. It is not just a matter of a few steps. If it were, it would have been sorted a long time ago. There will be setbacks, as there always are, and your child needs to feel you are in this together. You are not just watching on.

You need to be ready to think:
- What can we do about this?
- How can we help with this?
- How can we make it easier for you, while still moving forward?
- How can I help you to be brave and strong?

Spotting brave behaviour

Sometimes brave behaviour is very hard to notice. It can be the smallest of things, the tiniest of baby steps. But your child will be making progress. If your child has gone to school, and argued for seven minutes instead of ten minutes, or has tolerated a dog from a distance instead of close-up, they should be congratulated! You are not looking for the complete goal to be achieved. Any baby-step towards success should be acknowledged.

Learning to be brave and strong

Children and young adults need to be encouraged to be brave and internally strong in all behaviour that they find difficult. It is important to highlight that for each of us the 'things' are different.

Telling a child: "be brave and strong" will have little effect if said in an authoritarian style. As an order, it will not work. However, highlighting how I, as a parent or carer, need to be brave and strong, will model some of that behaviour for the child.

I'm Scared

You may describe a difficult day with a grumpy boss as: "She wanted me to do all this work, and I knew I couldn't do it! But I knew I had to be brave and strong!"

Remember to use this language carefully, because with over-use you will get classic eye-rolling and an instant look of boredom from your child. But, by using it just occasionally, you are giving the message, I am finding my stuff very tough and you are finding your stuff very tough. I respect you.

SUMMARY OF STEP FOUR

- It is hard to keep going. Everybody feels like giving up sometimes

- Break the fears into small, achievable steps (or stairs). The first stair can be something your child can already do

- Make a map of the stairs so your child can see that they are getting closer to success with their ultimate fear

- Build in some rewards for the hard work

- Look out for baby-steps that are marks of success

- Remember, it is important to get the balance right, just like juggling the accelerator and clutch of a manual car. Too much pushing means the child can be paralysed by fear and you are back at the beginning. Too much softly, softly and you are not moving forward

- Be aware of your own parenting style and its influence on your child. An anxious parent may demonstrate anxious behaviour. Modelling brave and strong behaviour is important

- Give the message to your child: we are in this together!

I'm Scared

STEP FIVE

Building resilience and further skills

BUILDING RESILIENCE AND FURTHER SKILLS

Fearing failure can drive anxiety

Fearing failure is one of the driving forces in anxiety. Whether it be the fear of failing to have a successful conversation (as in social anxiety) or the fear of failing to impress the school teacher with writing tasks, the fear can be overwhelming.

Sometimes the fear is simply the fear of anxiety symptoms. For anybody who has had a panic attack, the fear of another one can be overwhelming. Children are no different. The fear of the fear is enormous!

Learning to fail is a part of life

It is very hard for children to keep going when they are filled with the fear of failure. Not only do we need to calm the worries, but we also need to explain that learning to fail is a part of life. No one is successful throughout their lives. We all have smack-down moments, and moments of failure.

The Museum of Failure pioneered in Helsingborg, Sweden, and now located in several countries across the world, is a celebration of failure. The items displayed seemed like a good idea at the time but were complete failures. My favourite items are the Colgate

Lasagne, and Harley Davidson perfume, but there are many other spectacular failures as well.

At least one school in Melbourne has pioneered the idea of celebrating failure to make them feel more a part of life, and to lessen the overwhelming feeling of disaster.

In a week of festivity, teachers are asked to publicly acknowledge their failures to the school community. A challenging time for them no doubt, but a period of growth for the students, who learn that failure is not just a part of life, but also something from which you can recover.

Just like the knock-me-down toys that come bouncing back up, children need to learn how to bounce back when they *feel* they have failed, or indeed when they have 'failed' in some way.

Failure can help to build resilience

Fearing failure, and being paralysed by it, feeds anxiety. The anxiety can build and build. But if the fear of failure is calmed, and the anxiety reduced, failure can help to build resilience. Experiencing failure and learning to cope with it, is an important part of life — a most important part of building resilience.

Much has been made of resilience in recent times. Andrew Fuller, clinical psychologist, has described resilience as the ability to bungee jump through life. I love this description. Resilience is the ability to pick yourself up and keep going after hard times, sometimes very hard times.

I'm Scared

Everybody has trials and tribulations in life. Everybody has hard times. Granted, some people have harder times than others. But the hard times seem hard to everyone when they compare it to the rest of their life.

Coping with the tough knocks of life is one of the most difficult things to do. It doesn't matter what your age. Sometimes carers and parents have a tendency to feel, *If they can't cope with that, how will they cope with adult life?*

The implication is that tougher stuff is ahead without realising that given a young child's thoughts, feelings and abilities, this *is* the tough stuff! And conquering anxiety may be the hardest thing a child does in their entire life.

> Octavia was a young girl who delighted in everything to do with nature. She watched the ants making trails outside, treasured her bird-book from which she could identify local birds, and loved trips to the zoo.
>
> Her parents decided for her 7th birthday they would buy her a pet. They went to the pet-shop and carefully selected a goldfish with an attractive tank, stones and weed for the fish to nibble on.
>
> Octavia was thrilled with her new fish. She named it 'Mozart' because it seemed such a clever fish. It swam close to her whenever she came near, and she couldn't resist feeding it each time she saw him. She would say

> *hello to Mozart first thing each morning, and every night would say good-night.*
>
> *Unfortunately, Mozart was a clever fish. So much so that one day he leapt out of the tank. It was not till the afternoon that the family discovered the tragedy. Octavia was devastated. She cried and cried.*
>
> *Her family tried all sorts of things to cheer her up, going for an ice-cream, visiting a park, but nothing worked. Finally, in frustration, her mother yelled at her, "It was just a fish! We eat them all the time!"*
>
> *Of course, that upset Octavia even more. She became a vegetarian on the spot and refused to come out of her room for the rest of the day.*

It is devastating to lose a precious pet. Octavia's fish brought great joy, much fun and lots of happy times and even companionship. Suddenly it was gone. While an adult may see the whole experience as a minor event and say, "It was just a fish!", for the child this is their first experience of grief and loss. No one likes grief and loss.

Challenges for children and young people are everywhere

School work and homework can be one of the greatest challenges for children and young people. If a student is so anxious they're unable to tell the teacher they can't understand the work or can't ask for help, they may sit paralysed by fear. The world keeps moving on at a pace, and the young person is left behind, feeling more and more bewildered.

It gets to a point that when asked what they don't understand the student wants to scream "Everything!"

We all face challenges in life. It can be particularly valuable, however, in building resilience, especially if you are supported by your own personal cheer squad who will keep cheering you on no matter what.

Helicopter parent vs cheerleader parent

The term 'helicopter parent' was reportedly first suggested in the 1960s by Dr Haim Ginott, a psychologist and educator, to describe the overly-fussy parent who hovers over their child ensuring every step is safe, and no mistakes are made.

Clearly, to be described as a helicopter parent is not a compliment. And remember you don't have to be a parent to be a helicopter parent. Care-givers and grandparents can be helicopter parents too.

Yet, how do we know when we have found the right point where we allow children to fall and hurt themselves for a life-lesson rather

Step Five: Building resilience and further skills

than a catastrophic injury? Our children and young people are precious. We don't have a batch of others to practice on.

The desperate need of a loving parent is to protect and mend their children. Often wrapping children up in cotton wool seems like a *very* good idea.

But, it is important to distinguish here between a 'helicopter parent' and a 'cheerleader parent'. If we continue to use the cheer squad analogy, we realise the cheer squad doesn't get up and play the game, no matter how badly the team is playing. The cheer squad is there to yell: "Keep going, you've got this!", rather than "Let me play, I'm better than you!"

I'm Scared

I suspect, if you have ever supported a team that has lost badly, you know the feeling of wanting to run on to the field or pitch, but you are not allowed to! The same goes for teaching resilience... you have to let them fall. The good cheerleader parent will cheer on through the darkest of times, through the toughest of times, without taking over. And never is this more necessary than with the anxious child.

> *The following example is my own:*
>
> *As a young nine-year-old girl, I lived in a village in Switzerland, just outside Basel. At school, in Year 3, the German language was spoken in the classroom, and Swiss-German spoken in the playground, a little confusing for short-stay foreigners from Australia.*
>
> *Mostly my schoolwork and homework were modified so that I did not need to do as much as everyone else. But one day, probably a day the teacher was feeling a little cross and grumpy, she set us all the task of memorising a 14-line German poem, called Die Heinzelmännchen, overnight.*
>
> *When I asked what my modified work would be, she told me I would memorise it like everyone else. I went home and cried and cried. I was fearful of the teacher and feared failing so publicly. I was completely overwhelmed.*
>
> *My parents consoled me, and then my father insisted I could do this. He would help me by translating the entire poem into English and then we would memorise it together in German. And we did!*

> *I wasn't called on to recite the poem, but I had arrived at school feeling brave and strong, and thinking, I've got this!*
>
> *It was the hardest thing I have done in my life, and was only successful because of the supportive and collaborative nature of my parents. They didn't rescue me. They didn't write a letter to the teacher to save me.*
>
> *That would have been a much easier option. For all of us.*

It takes courage to persist in hard times

For children, failure (or near-failure) seems such a disaster. Whether it be making mathematical errors, or misspelling a word, failure can seem like all is lost. To the young child, it can seem like there is no point in continuing if he or she is only going to fail again.

But the challenge is often not the task itself, but the thinking around the problem. Coming up with helpful thoughts is tough. Encouraging children to be brave and strong during the tough times is one of the hardest tasks of a parent or carer.

Sometimes everyday examples of modern-day heroes can help children to persevere through thick and thin. The world is full of entrepreneurs and 'disruptors', many of whom have persevered through tough times. JK Rowling reportedly submitted *Harry Potter and the Philosopher's Stone* to 12 different publishers only to be rejected by all. The book was finally accepted by Bloomsbury, and went on to sell over 500 million books. And I'm guessing the publishers who rejected it have never lived it down.

WD-40 spray, used for the lubrication of locks, was created by scientists with the '40', supposedly the 40th attempt at getting it right. And, in Australia, the Victorian Ararat Eagles reserves football team had not won a football game for around four years. It seems no one could quite remember how long it was since they had won, and yet, everyone kept playing. Now that's resilience!

The mark of success for all these people is that they have never given up. They keep working through tough times, they don't let the hard times defeat them.

And so, for children, how not to give up is the real challenge. Normalising failure is the first part, and then encouraging perseverance is next.

There are several mantras, like those outlined in Step 3, that are helpful here. These include:

- When the going gets tough, the tough get going
- Fall down seven times, get up eight times
- Never, ever, give up
- If at first you don't succeed, try, try again

WHAT TO SAY

We have worked out it is so easy to get things wrong. Usually, people get things wrong every day.

Sometimes the weather forecast is wrong. They said it would rain and it didn't.

Sometimes, we forget where we put something. Remember when I couldn't find my … *(eg. keys/wallet/phone)*, **and we all had to search for it?**

Usually, kids, young people and grown-ups get some things wrong at school.

There is even a museum in Sweden dedicated to failure. Let's have a look at the website and see if we can find what has failed.
The website is *www.museumoffailure.com*

Elsa loved school from the start. By the time she was in Year 2, she loved catching up with her friend and playing on the monkey bars at lunchtime. She adored her young teacher. Much to her mother's annoyance, anything Miss Clark asked for, she got. Anything Elsa's mother asked for was carefully considered, and a cost-benefit analysis drawn up.

But as the year progressed Elsa became more and more reluctant to attend school. She had stomach pains and headaches galore, with no real sickness evident. Her mother began to wonder what was going on.

One evening Elsa was in floods of tears, and admitted she was letting Miss Clark down. She had completely failed Miss Clark. She got some sums wrong, and had misspelt one word in the spelling test.

No matter how much Elsa's mother tried to explain mistakes were a part of learning, Elsa continued in great distress. She had failed the person who was most important in her life!

Elsa's mother considered 'most important in her life' a bit strong! But biting her tongue, she suggested they meet with Miss Clark and discuss how Elsa had let her down. All the time knowing full well that Miss Clark probably hadn't even noticed.

Elsa was very reluctant to take this action, but Elsa's mother said she would be meeting with Miss Clark either way, so Elsa might as well come along.

Step Five: Building resilience and further skills

> *Before school, the pair met with Miss Clark who assured Elsa that not only was it okay to make mistakes, but she expected mistakes, as that showed students were pushing themselves.*
>
> *Miss Clark suggested that they look through her work to find all the mistakes so they could celebrate how hard Elsa was pushing herself. Elsa was delighted and again became the happy schoolgirl she had been. Only now she was comfortable to make mistakes from time to time.*

For Elsa, any mistake was a disaster, especially if it was for the teacher she adored. She became fearful of making mistakes and her anxiety grew into physical symptoms.

Elsa's mother was impressive. She did not take offence at Elsa's adoration for her teacher. She put aside her own feelings to cheer on her daughter, but also helped her daughter to solve the problem. With a little support in going to see the teacher, and having a plan, the anxiety melted away.

No doubt, Elsa was still anxious in tests, and worried about clear marks of pass or fail, but in day-to-day activities she could manage her anxiety just fine.

Is our language helpful or hopeless?

The way we talk to ourselves can be harsh. Really harsh. In fact, sometimes we speak more rudely to ourselves than we would to a friend or neighbour.

Sometimes the language we use to ourselves, when we think we are failing, is awful. Children and young people are no different.

What a loser! Why don't I get that? Everyone else gets it! I am such a dunder-head! These are all common themes and thoughts for children, particularly when prone to anxiety.

Rapee et al (2008) points out that anxious children are often rigid in their thoughts. Children cannot think around a problem. They just get stuck in their thoughts with no other alternatives possible.

Children may think that everybody — truly everybody — except for them gets the math equation. There are no allowances made — some people get it, some people don't. They do not allow for the possibility of different degrees of understanding. Their thoughts seem to be in black and white. It either is, or it isn't, there is no in-between to them.

And the thinking tends to go...

They get it. I don't. Therefore, I am a loser.

This is a simple equation played out in a child's mind the world over. The assumption is justified, and it seems hard to find a reason to keep on trying. If I am the loser of the race, it doesn't matter whether I quit now or keep going. I have still lost. So, why keep going?

Giving a sense of hope

But this kind of hopeless language perpetuates the feeling of failure and disaster, and feeds the anxiety. By changing the language to be more hopeful, the child or young person gets a sense that some change is possible. If the child changes, "I can't do this" to "I can't do this, *yet*", there is a sense of hope. If we turn, "I will mess this up" into "Everyone messes up, sometimes", there is hope.

Children and young people always need a sense of hope. A hope that things will get better, especially when life is feeling bleak or overwhelming. However, the challenge is: *How do we give this sense of hope?*

Mantras can be extremely useful in developing hopeful thinking. They can be repeated over and over, and called upon even when under great stress. Check back to the mantras suggested in Step 3, but *"When I stay calm I think better" and "I've done it before, I can do it again"*, are two of my favourites.

Developing masterful thinking

In *Mindset: Changing the way you think to fulfil your potential*, Carol Dweck promotes the concept of the growth mindset. She argues we need to understand that our ability is something that can grow rather than something static, where it is just programmed into us.

She describes the fixed mindset of thinking where our skills are assumed to be set in concrete and characterised by rigid thoughts. With the growth mindset, we achieve more by thinking around problems. A fixed mindset is an unhelpful approach to the world, she argues.

A person with a fixed mindset focuses on their smart skills and knowledge but does not cope well with challenges or unpredictability. The fixed mindset ignores criticism or takes it as a condemnation rather than seeing it as constructive feedback. Dweck points out the person's potential for growth is then limited.

However, with a growth mindset a talent can be strengthened with hard work. Challenges are an opportunity for growth. Mistakes are just another way of learning. People with a growth mindset can thrive and reach their full potential. People with a fixed mindset cannot.

So, it is not pre-programmed in the stars that we are bad at math, our skills can be improved by hard work. For this reason, it is unhelpful for parents to provide comments to their children like *"Our family is always bad at math"*. Talk about a get out of jail free card! The message is: *"Don't worry it is written in the stars that you won't be able to do this. Don't even try!"*

A much more helpful, and hopeful message is, *"I struggled at math, but I found by doing (use example) it really helped."*

Fortunately, many teachers are aware of the growth mindset, and promote it well, but it is also important that these skills are encouraged at home.

WHAT TO SAY

Nobody can be good at everything, except maybe super heroes. We all have things that are hard for us.

I find... *(eg. staying calm when I am worried/playing sports/doing math/meeting new people)* **hard. It is really difficult for me.**

It does not mean I am going to be hopeless at it for the rest of my life. It just means this is something for me to work on. And I will keep struggling to do it.

Sometimes I make really stupid mistakes. But that's okay. Sometimes I need some help to make things better. That's okay too.

At pre-school, Jarryd loved counting and drawing pictures. He was great at building sand castles and riding tricycles and was generally a bundle of energy.

Commencing school was not a problem. He thought his teacher was very clever, and he always wanted to please her. The first year was a cinch.

But as he progressed through school he started to struggle with math. He could count well, but had trouble putting the numbers together. He didn't understand the concept of addition let alone subtraction. Why was it so hard?

At home, the happy, bouncy boy had become angry and withdrawn. His parents were wondering what was going on. One day, while walking to school, Jarryd spilled the beans. He just couldn't do math. Everyone else got it, but he didn't.

His teacher liked him, he was sure of that. He didn't want to upset her or stop her from liking him. He was sure she wouldn't like someone who couldn't do math.

His father reassured Jarryd. "This will be okay," he said. His teacher would keep liking him, especially as he had been trying hard. He offered to speak to the teacher to explain how much Jarryd didn't understand.

> Then his father explained to Jarryd, "I struggled at math. It was hard for me, but I found I just needed to find a different way to learn it. Maybe we could talk to the teacher and see if there is another way of learning this. Maybe we could find a tutor who can explain it differently. We just need to approach this differently. That's what I needed to do, and it helped a lot. And it all worked out fine."
>
> His father gave him a wink. "This will all work out fine for you, too!"

Balancing fun and worries

An anxious child is often perceived as a very serious child, rarely showing a sense of fun or happiness. But, it is hard to be happy when you think disaster is about to befall you at every turn. It is hard to be happy when you feel like you are going to vomit from worries.

Sometimes it will be important for parents to make a conscious effort to bring more fun into their child's life. Scheduling activities that focus on family fun can be as simple as going to a park and playing with a ball or playing a board game.

Laughing at the stupid things we do can contribute to having a more relaxed, resilient approach to the world. Encourage your child to understand life is about having fun, and that there is more to life than winning or losing. When we laugh at our own mistakes, the child or young person can learn it is okay to make mistakes. It's okay to fail.

We hope our children can at least learn from their mistakes, even if they can't be proud of them. We want them to be able to laugh at themselves. So, parents, grandparents, and significant others need to demonstrate that laughter when we have made mistakes of our own.

But, it is very important to note here that you are NOT laughing at your child's or young person's mistakes. That would be shameful and dispiriting for them. Your job is to laugh at *your* mistakes, and to keep modelling mistakes happen in the modern world, and I am okay with that.

Our fear of looking stupid sometimes overrides this ability to laugh at ourselves. When we have done something stupid, we are not inclined to share our stupidity. But that is exactly what I am asking you to do. Have a laugh at yourself, but not your child or young person.

I'm Scared

Minnie was a fashion-conscious 18 year old. Her sense of design and colour was enviable. When her eyesight deteriorated a little, she needed to wear glasses. She seemed to have an amazing supply of glasses to match each outfit she was wearing.

In her never-ending quest to find the perfect glasses to match her outfits, she regularly visited eye wear specialists. For some people, she argued, there is a desire for shoes, for others — like her — it was a desire for glasses.

On one occasion, she could not find the right fit, the right match and the right colour. She tried on nearly all the glasses in the store. At last, she settled on a pair that were lying on the counter. They were perfect. They fitted well, were a great colour, and looked great.

Imagine her dismay when she asked to buy them, only to discover they were her very own. She had forgotten which model she was wearing!

Instead of worrying what the sales staff thought and slinking out of the shop, she shared a laugh with them. She admitted her own mistake, shared the 'failure' to recognise her own glasses and continued to tell the story at her own expense, with her friends and family.

Minnie now realised this was just another step in her journey in developing resilience. She was laughing at her mistakes, just like her parents' laughed at their own mistakes.

Sometimes anxious behaviour looks like bad behaviour

It is very common for children who are highly anxious to look like they are being naughty or obstinate. They refuse to do an activity. They refuse to complete their homework. They refuse to mix with other children.

Sometimes it is clear the behaviour is driven by anxiety, but sometimes it is not. Usually you can assume that if they are not going out to play with friends, some sort of anxiety or bullying is going on.

So, how do you tell the difference between naughty behaviour and anxious behaviour? One of the best ways is to consider the behaviour carefully and to offer support. Often, it is important to think about the purpose or function of the behaviour. If the purpose of the behaviour is to gain attention, it is unlikely to be driven by anxiety.

On the other hand, if the behaviour is designed to avoid something, anxiety may be the driving force in the behaviour.

Come on, I will help you!

Often by offering to support a child or young person to do a task, they will complete it. For instance, if the child is refusing to clean the room, they will often agree to having help.

Sometimes, the child may be feeling tired and lazy and just reluctant to clean the room. Yes, we all have those days. But if the child is insistent they can't go into the room, even with help, then maybe the behaviour is driven by worry. Strong fear is usually evident to family members, but occasionally a child or young person can hide it well.

If they are adamant no matter what the reward, no matter whether they are given help, they still can't do it, you can guess anxiety is at work. If they lap up the reward or are enthusiastic about help and seem to leave all the work to you, then you have been conned! Next time you won't be fooled. Don't get angry, just remind yourself that you won't be falling for that trick again!

Donnie was your typical five year old who would not go to bed. But lately, every night when it was time for bed, he would tantrum.

His parents were so frustrated. As soon as the night-time routine started with a bath, he would become grumpy. As he put on his pyjamas, he looked angry, and by the time he had listened to a story he would start screaming. His parents scolded him, practised tough love, and on one occasion held the door closed until he fell asleep. Nothing helped.

This went on for a week until, at the suggestion of their friend, they tried talking to Donnie about what made it so hard to go to bed. Donnie explained he was terrified of the monsters under the bed. He hadn't mentioned this to his parents, and he did not talk about monsters, so they weren't to know. But his friends at school had told him monsters were there. They described how they would come out when he went to sleep. Poor boy lay terrified as he waited for sleep.

Once his parents realised what was going on they explained monsters were not real. For several days they took turns lying with him until he went to sleep. With careful soothing from his parents, and a lot of comfort, he gradually returned to sleeping by himself.

Bed-time was never his favourite time, but Donnie learned to 'manage' it successfully.

Building skills

In business, a lot of work has been done for adults in the area of skill-building. Much focus has been put on setting goals and measuring what can be achieved. Psychological studies have been done in numerous organisations to determine what helps to build skills, and what helps to build a successful organisation. Many authors have focused on visualising what success will look like and how it will be achieved.

So how can we use this feeling of success with children? After all, children who have learned to be successful are likely to feel more confident. With the increased confidence they may have a sense they can conquer their fears. This does not mean they have eliminated their worries and fears, but it can mean they have a sense of, *this will turn out all right!*

Setting goals for striving forward

Daydreaming about being an Olympic swimmer can be a useful way to set a goal, but if I am aged over 30, and have never really enjoyed swimming, the chances of me reaching my goal are zilch. No matter how much I dream about it or picture it in my head, I will not reach that goal. It is totally unrealistic to think I can.

Setting goals for children needs to be something realistic for them, and something important to them. Not something important to the parent, or carer. For the parent, the goal may be for the child to get better at tidying his or her room. For the child, this is very, very low on the list of priorities!

To achieve success, the goal needs to be small and achievable. And something the child would like to achieve. So, forget room cleaning for the moment.

Fortunately, schools often have goal setting as part of the curriculum, so setting a goal is not a foreign concept to children. There are often skills a child may want to improve, whether it be dancing, acting or basketball, or getting better at math, handwriting or art. When setting goals start small and aim for something that is important to them.

Setting a goal

For whatever goal has been set, it is important to keep it simple and to be clear:

- What: is required
- How: it will be practised
- When: it will be achieved

It is also very important to be clear about what success looks like. How will you know when you have reached the goal? How will you measure it? How will you know when to celebrate?

Small steps are key

In working with anxiety, small steps are key. Whether it is providing challenges, as in the stairs up the mountain in Step 4, or setting goals to strive forward, it is by setting achievable mini-bites that a child or young person's confidence grows.

So, getting better at math is a great goal, but way too tough. How do you know *when* you have got there? How do you know when you have 'got better'? And how do you know when it is 'enough'?

And so, the goal needs to be clearly articulated. It needs to state what will be done and *when*. I will practice my six-times tables for math every Friday night is a great goal. I will get better at math, not so much.

By stating when and what time practice will occur, success is more likely. Focus on this single goal and forget all the other components of mathematics that need to be worked on. For the moment, only the six-times tables are important.

WHAT TO SAY

When things are hard for us, or they get tough, we make a plan to help change things.

Step Five: Building resilience and further skills

> We made a plan for the worries, and we will keep working on them.
>
> Sometimes it is good to work on something else we would like to get better at so you can feel stronger and more confident.
>
> Is there anything you would like to get better at?
>
> (If there is a skill that is easy to teach, work on it. If there is nothing, don't try to create things. Working on worries is hard enough.)

Setting bright lines is useful

The concept of a bright line in psychological work was first introduced to me by Owain Service and Rory Gallagher in their book, *Think Small: the surprisingly simple ways to reach big goals*. The 'bright line' indicates the boundary line for a plan, or rule, to show when you have failed.

In football or tennis when the ball is over the line it is out. Now there may be some argument from the players about whether it is over the line, but it is generally agreed that once it is over the line it is out. The bright line works in the same way. When the bright line is crossed, the plan has not been followed. The rules of the plan have not been obeyed.

If I say I will practice my times tables every Friday night, it is clear by Saturday morning whether I have done it or not. If I didn't practise on Friday night, and even if I practised lots on Saturday, I crossed the bright line. The bright line makes it clear I did not follow what was planned.

Sometimes it can be useful to have consequences for crossing a bright line. This can be light-hearted, but reminds the child the task wasn't completed. It is best for the child to choose the consequence for themselves. Often, they are very good at choosing quite severe consequences, but some examples might be:

- Wearing the clothes of a sibling
- Wearing the opposition team's football jumper
- Cheering for the opposition at a sporting venue
- Foregoing a favourite treat (eg. dessert)
- Allowing a sibling or parent to determine all screen games to be played for the day

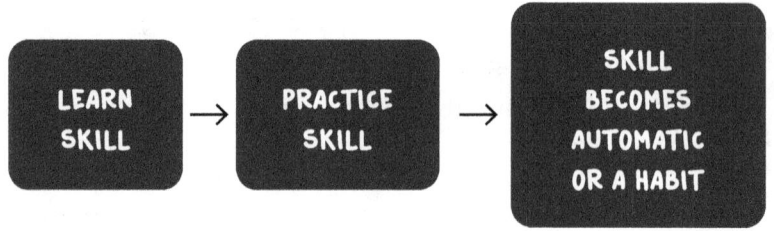

Creating great habits

To achieve success with these goals, habits need to be created. By focusing on habits and achieving goals we are building strength and confidence in the young person.

The where, when, and how of the goal will begin to create a habit or routine. By practising over and over without crossing the bright line, the child or young adult begins to incorporate the behaviour into everyday life.

Sometimes it is important to remind children and young people they do not have to concentrate carefully about where and how they move their legs and feet. Walking has become an automatic skill for most.

For young children still learning to do up buttons, it is an onerous chore to put on a shirt with buttons. For the rest of us, we decide on our shirt according to the weather rather than whether it has buttons or not.

> **WHAT TO SAY**
>
> You probably don't remember when you were learning to walk, but I do. To start with, you would hold onto furniture or someone's hands to stand up.
>
> Gradually you would take a couple of steps and then fall over. Sometimes you would decide to get somewhere it was easier to crawl. But other times you would stand up and move around, carefully moving your leg, and balancing.
>
> I wonder if we have any video clips of you learning to walk. It was such an exciting time. And you just kept trying. It's amazing to remember it.
>
> Now, you don't even need to think about it. It is just automatic.

Skills like smiling, crawling and talking seem to be pre-programmed into the human body. For babies born at term, it takes around six weeks before they smile. But it takes a 35-week premature baby five weeks to reach term, and then another six weeks to smile — a total of eleven weeks.

While some skills are developmental or automatic, plenty of other skills are not. Just ask the parent of a teenager who has been asked to clean their bedroom. Or the grandparent asking the young person to leave the computer and come and help with chores. Learning to complete household chores is not an automatic skill, it needs to be learned, and usually not very willingly.

Mostly, children and young people don't want doing chores or hard work to become automatic. They just don't want to do them in the first place!

All they see is hard work, and when they are tired after school they have little energy left for learning. Remember, it is tiring to learn, and tiring to grow. And teenagers, particularly, are doing a lot of both. If you asked anybody to urgently do a task after running a marathon, chances are they would not want to do it. So, doing chores is probably not the place to start in developing new skills for confidence and bravery.

It takes planning, time, and practice to turn skills into habits or into routines that are done automatically.

> **WHAT TO SAY**
>
> Sometimes other things we do can become automatic too. Some children don't need to think about how to get ready for bed. They just know they need to put on pyjamas, brush their teeth, read a book and get into bed.
>
> Wow, four steps that have just been rolled into one thing: going to bed.
>
> There are all sorts of things we can make automatic by practising them more. Once it is automatic, you don't even need to think about it.
>
> For you, walking is automatic. Talking is automatic. But there are other things that aren't automatic.

Timing is important

As you will understand if you have ever told a joke badly, or dropped a catch, timing is everything. And, as you have probably worked out by now, timing is everything when delivering a message to your child or young person.

If you ask the young person to come to the dinner table just as they are about to reach the next level on a computer game, or as they have reached the climax of their story, they are unlikely to come immediately. But, if you had asked a couple of minutes later you may have had instant compliance.

When choosing to talk about developing habits, choose your timing carefully. Perhaps a family meeting, or when you are out driving or taking a walk together, would be a good time to have a conversation about 'how can I help you' to develop these skills. It is important to highlight these habits are to help develop strength and confidence, and of your child's choosing, not your own.

The worst time to suggest habits are needed is when a parent is angry. The child or young person is likely to flatly refuse to work on a skill because it is important to the adult, the angry adult. There will be no buy-in at all.

Choosing habits to work on

When devising the plan for habits, choose something important to the child or young person. Children may see getting ready for school in the morning so you don't nag them, as important. Likewise, so they don't have to go the office to get a late pass. But, unless you have an overly generous child, 'helping me to get to work on time' will not be a good enough reason to work on the habit.

Cues and habits

Cues can be very important in developing habits. Sometimes having a visual reminder of the steps involved can be invaluable. Many parents will be familiar with the tick-chart used to prepare for school.

✓ GET UP
✓ SHOWER
✓ GET DRESSED
✓ HAVE BREAKFAST
✓ BRUSH TEETH
✓ BRUSH HAIR
✓ PACK BAG
✓ PLAY GAME

Cues can be a visual reminder, or situational, or sometimes even a sound, that reminds you or your child that action needs to be taken. For instance, I may leave a note on the bench as a reminder to call a friend, I may go to the fridge for food whenever I sit down on the couch to watch a movie, or I may start to get ready for bed when my phone alarm goes off.

It is important to understand what cues are working for us, and what cues are working against us. The cue to practice the six-times tables will be completely undone if you are sitting in the family room on a Friday night where movies are usually watched. The cue to watch movies is very strong, and the habit of practising the six-times tables won't even get started!

Be sympathetic in helping your child or young person to develop habits. Only start with one, and recognise it is very hard to get started. Incorporate positive cues to assist with the task and eliminate any negative cues or associations.

> **WHAT TO SAY**
>
> **Is there anything else you would like to make automatic, so you don't need to think about it?**
>
> **We could work out what we want to turn into an automatic skill, or habit.**
>
> **Something that you would be able to do quickly and without even thinking about.** *(Suggest something, but make sure it will help your child, not you.)*
>
> **Maybe getting ready for school, so you aren't late?**
>
> **Maybe practising math, so you are like those tables champs you have been talking about?**
> *(Choose something easy to work on.
> This is important, so you can be successful.)*

Why help with habits?

So, your child has nominated a skill they would like to work on. You have helped to decide on the practice needed. For the habit to develop, you will need to practice over and over again. Sometimes, it is hard to practice when someone is tired and has poor concentration after school. Choose your times carefully.

By practising regularly and developing it into a habit, the young person becomes more confident and comfortable with the task.

The more concrete habits that can be developed, the less 'thinking' time that is spent doing them. Doing homework quickly and at a prescribed time can be useful. Managing to do it as a habit means that there is no dawdling, no inward struggle, and no constant arguing. Otherwise, the time spent on argument can be longer than doing the task itself.

Building habits using rewards

For the practice to turn into habits, sometimes rewards need to be added. A dishwasher can often be emptied within 5-7 minutes, depending on the size of the hand of the child or young person, and the size of the kitchen. The bigger the hand, the easier it is to balance a collection of plates or bowls together. The larger the kitchen the more steps that need to be taken to reach the cupboard that stores the crockery. For some children, each bowl must be collected individually and walked to the cupboard.

But, each child may be able to reach a personal best (PB) time for emptying the dishwasher, with big penalties for breakages, to reduce cracking and chipping. By focusing on the PB the child no longer focuses on the chore, and the difficulty in completing it.

> **WHAT TO SAY**
>
> Remember, we want this to become an automatic habit, like walking. So, we need to do lots of practice.
>
> And I'm thinking to do lots of practice, you will need someone to be the coach, like in football, some goals and maybe some rewards.
>
> Well, it seems that if we can turn it into a habit, you will feel happier, and feel confident about doing these things.
>
> Now, let's work out what we have to do…
>
> What would you like to work on? And how will we know you have succeeded?
>
> Who do you want as your everyday coach? It's okay if it isn't me.

> When do you want to practice?
>
> What do you think will stop the practice from happening?
>
> What can we do about that?
>
> And the best part of all, what could be a reward for getting this done?

Putting it all together

By planning for the things that will get in the way, we are planning for success. There are always things that will get in the way. If getting ready for school is the habit, having a late night, or getting up late, stops the success.

By recognising these 'interrupters' we can find a way to work around them. By acknowledging that things get in the way, the child does not give up at the first hurdle.

As success is achieved, the child or young person has a feeling that they can win at this, and resilience grows.

The power of self-control

Many people are familiar with what is often called the 'marshmallow test', set by psychologists at Stanford University many years ago (Mischel et al, 1972). In it, three-and-a-half to 5-year-old children were offered something nice to eat, like a marshmallow or pretzel. They were told that they could choose to eat their least preferred treat, but if they waited (for a 15-minute period) they would get both treats. The tester then left the room. In some of the experiments children were encouraged to play with toys, or to think of fun things as a distraction. Interestingly, the children who thought of fun things waited for longer than the children who played with toys and thought about the rewards. Of course, some children did not find the task so difficult, simply waiting, while others ate the treat immediately.

Later studies suggested children who were able to wait for the reward of two treats, no matter their age, tended to have better life outcomes, as measured by school results and other 'life' measures.

It seems the power of self-control is a very important skill in life. And it makes sense. If I can plan my life rather than *react* to life, I am likely to be more successful.

The Dunedin Multidisciplinary Health and Development Study (Dunedin Study) is another life-time study of the health and development and well-being of over 1000 New Zealand children and babies born in the Dunedin area, with follow-up every two to three years.

An American study, using the New Zealand findings, by Moffitt et al., (2011), also showed greater success across various life areas when children demonstrated self-control. In other words, it was the child's ability for self-control, separate from their intelligence, social class and 'dumb' mistakes made as adolescents that predicted their success in life.

So, does it mean all is lost if my child cannot develop self-control? Not at all, it just means some children may need to work a little harder on it, than others.

For some children, sitting in class is simple. For others, they may have to focus hard on paying attention to the teacher, trying to ignore all the distractions they are seeing. Developing self-control takes time and practice.

Teaching self-control

We all know how hard it is to use self-control. Just ask the person on a diet, or the New Year resolutioners. How many ways can it all go awry? Lots!

Some children find self-control harder than others. And certainly, younger children find it especially hard. So, how can we coax it along in our children? By realistic practice.

It is important to identify your child's skills in waiting and putting off what is pleasurable to them. Do they eat their Easter Eggs all at once? Or, do they make them last until the next month? If they are making them last till the end of the month, they already have good self-control.

Do they insist a play-date happens today? Or, can they wait until tomorrow or later in the week? The child who can wait already has self-control.

Should we work on this skill?

Sometimes parents are aware their child has more difficulty waiting than most. It is important to remember it is a skill that develops over time, so don't have unrealistic expectations. A younger child can't do what an older child can. Some children walk sooner than others, some talk sooner than others. It is not a race, and usually it evens out in the end.

But, if your child is having much more difficulty waiting than his or her friends, it may be worth practising some waiting skills. Waiting is very hard for most children (and adults), especially if you don't have access to a smartphone. No, I am not advocating everyone be given smartphones, but I am acknowledging waiting in a boring environment is harder than waiting in an entertaining one. It is no surprise that children have trouble waiting in a supermarket if there are no activities for them!

If you are wanting to build these skills, there are a variety of ways to encourage them. Self-control is generally about learning to sit with discomfort. For children, this discomfort comes in various forms: the discomfort of having nothing to do, the discomfort of waiting for adults to stop talking, and the discomfort of waiting for a turn during a game, are just a few.

There are all sorts of ways of building these skills, but basically the aim is to just make that uncomfortable feeling last a little longer. Just like balancing the accelerator and the clutch in Step 4, a child needs to learn how to tolerate that uncomfortable feeling for just a little longer.

But, if you push too hard, and ask them to wait for a long time, you will go straight back to the beginning again, with little enthusiasm for starting over.

For some children, waiting for 30 seconds is an extraordinary painful task, for some it is not. By practising 'strong sitting' with a straight back, hands in the lap and not talking, a child can learn to extend some waiting time, and learn to put up with 'uncomfortable'" just a little longer. Remember, this is just one way to encourage waiting skills.

After all, there are plenty of ways to teach this skill:

- Playing board games, and needing to wait for a turn (more than one player)
- Visiting a toy at the toy shop for several days (or longer) before it is purchased
- Going fishing
- Playing *Pass the Parcel*, *Guess Who* or any other game that requires waiting
- Counting down the days to Christmas/holiday season with an Advent Calendar or calendar

WHAT TO SAY

Let's try a game of strong sitting.

This is something that you can learn to get better at, and it will help you at school, too.

What I want you to do is sit cross-legged on the floor. Now put your hands in your lap.

I am going to time how long you can sit with a straight back, without talking.

Go! *(start the timer)*

Great work! *(Praise the child, no matter how long they have managed.)*

I wonder if we could try it again?

(If your child says no, don't push it.)

Important note:
If you are not having success, give up. If your child does not find this 'game' interesting, give up. If your child cannot sit for 10 seconds, give up. There is no point in forcing your child to practice strong sitting, it will just destroy your relationship with them.

SUMMARY OF STEP FIVE

- Be a cheerleader parent/carer not a helicopter parent/carer

- Don't take life too seriously, search for fun to balance the worries

- Encourage perseverance as it helps to build resilience

- Set goals that can become habits

- Goals and habit may help a child to feel more confident in themselves

- Set goals that are meaningful to the young person, not you

- Practise, practise, practise so the skill becomes automatic and a habit

- Self-control is an important skill for children to learn

What else can I do?

WHAT ELSE CAN I DO?

So, you have the key 5 steps and hopefully, by now, you feel like you know what you are doing. But, what else can you do?

Sometimes, I liken a child's constant search for anxiety-provoking situations to be like a heat-seeking missile. It scans the environment, finds the target and locks on. Nothing can persuade these children to look away. Nothing can persuade these children they haven't found what they have been looking for — some catastrophic event. Nothing will convince them that this target — a world changing catastrophe — is not going to happen.

The power of gratitude

Some recent psychological work has focused on positive psychology, in which children and young people's strengths and virtues are focused on rather than what's not going right. By building these strengths along with feelings of safety, we may be able to reduce the sensation of fear and anxiety.

Likewise, by focusing on what is going well in the world, the child or young person may be less inclined to focus on the disasters. Sometimes, by writing down three great things that happened in the day, or three gratitudes, there can be a small change in focus.

The important thing to remember is that the 'great thing' may be small: I had yummy grapes in my lunchbox, my friend chose to be my partner at group-time, and my dog wagged its tail when I got home, are but a few.

The aim of listing gratitudes is to notice the small things in life, the small *good* things, instead of the impending disasters. The disasters have a .00001% chance of happening, the gratitudes are happening every day. It is time to start noticing the good instead of the doom and gloom.

> **WHAT TO SAY**
>
> I know you are an expert at spotting the worries, but now we are going to become experts at spotting the good things that happen in a day.
>
> Sometimes, it is easy to remember the bad things even if they didn't happen, but we don't remember the good things.
>
> Well, we might remember the big good things, like birthdays, but we don't remember the little good things.

> Now, we are going to notice three things that went well.
>
> But, that doesn't mean like winning selection to the national team in some sport, although that would be nice. It means like:
>
> It was a sunny day
> I got to finish my homework in class
> Jesse wanted to play with me
> I had a nice apple for lunch
>
> What three things can you think of today:
>
> 1.
> 2.
> 3.
>
> Shall we write them down somewhere so we can remember them?

By building gratitudes, the child starts to look for positives instead of negatives through the day. Hopefully, in searching for the positives, there is not so much time to notice the worries or dangers in the world.

Tool-box of strategies

Sometimes it is useful to have a tool-box of strategies that you can pull out at a moment's notice. Most of these strategies are not effective as a one-off or by themselves, but coupled with the 5 Steps, and sometimes with careful consideration about when to use them, they can be hugely successful.

The following strategies have been tried by some parents who swear by their success. However, it is important to highlight that many have no scientific basis or evidence-based reason for success. But perhaps there is a placebo effect. The child thinks it will work, so it will.

What are you looking forward to?

One tool for the tool-box is asking a simple question: "What are you looking forward to tomorrow?" Again, by trying to change the focus from the negative to the positive, you are trying to convince the child or young person to look for the fun things instead of rigidly thinking about the bad. But if your child insists there is nothing to look forward to you may need to make some suggestion. Be prepared!

Talking time

Setting up a specific time for talking can be particularly useful for the child or young person who worries a lot at night. By having a regular time during the day, it emphasises two things. Firstly, I care enough about you to put aside fifteen minutes in my very busy day. Secondly, let's worry about these things together so we can shoot down the unhelpful thoughts and plan some helpful thoughts.

What would you tell a friend?

Sometimes, a child or young person can come up with very rational thoughts when thinking about what they would tell a friend when they had a similar worry. Often, they are less rigid and less insistent that disaster is imminent, and come up with fabulous strategies, or at least repeat your suggested strategies. So, you find they have been listening!

Worry dolls

Worry dolls are thought to have originated from Guatemala and Mexico. Children would tell their worries to different dolls at night and then the dolls were put away in a box, with the theory that the dolls would solve the worries. Sometimes, the power of suggestion works well, sometimes it doesn't.

Creating a worry box

A worry-box can work in a similar way to worry dolls. The child or young person writes the worry down and then posts it into a box.

Throwing away the worries

Similar strategies including tearing up or destroying the paper on which it is written. Great drama can be created when destroying the paper, such as burning it, or throwing it away, and watching the garbage truck destroy it. Even imagining sending the worry into the sky can be successful.

Anxiety drops or pastilles

Some parents suggest specific anxiety drops and pastilles, such as Rescue Remedy™, have helped to calm their children when they are stressed. Similar effects have been suggested by smelling aromatherapy oils, or the use of lavender.

Managing scary dreams

Nightmares can be associated with anxiety. Sometimes talking through issues before bedtime can help. Another technique is when a distressed child wakes, is to shoo away the bad dreams, or monsters, out from under the bed, out from the wardrobe, and from anywhere else they may be hiding.

When do I call for professional help?

It is hard to know when to call the mental health professional. But some key indicators are:

- If the anxiety is linked to a specific traumatic event
- If the anxiety appears to be getting worse
- If you have tried to help but there has been little effect

If the above situations occur, it is time to call in the professionals. Sometimes, sooner rather than later is better. If the anxieties have been allowed to build and build, it is harder to bring them down.

How do I find someone who will be a good match for my child?

A good mental health professional will vary as much as children vary. A firm, forthright approach may suit one child or young adult, but not another. A quiet, gentle approach can be excellent for some children, but others may just take it as a signal to play in every session.

It is important to ensure the professional has had experience in working with children and young people and knows how to engage them. If rapport isn't built from the outset, success is a long way off.

If the child or young person is angry about attending sessions, it may be time to look for an alternative therapist. Nothing much can be achieved with a resistant client, young or old.

Despite what people think, parents will discuss good therapeutic experiences with other parents, so it may be worth asking friends for personal recommendations. Sometimes, children or young people will make recommendations to each other. How that comes up in playground conversation, I am still trying to work out!

Final words

If you have read this far, I am impressed. The experience of a parent of an anxious child is exhausting and distressing. Sometimes, parents feel like they have done their day's work before they even get to work. Sometimes, they just want to curl up into a ball and make the world stop.

One of the most important aspects of this book is to remember: don't feed into the stress. Your job is to stay calm and centred when the child is very anxious. Otherwise they will think: *see, there is a reason to be stressed!!!!*

Some studies have indicated that when the mother's anxiety was treated, the child's anxiety reduced. It is vital then, that you consider the language you use, and the discussions you have around current world events. Their minds are like heat-seeking missiles searching for the target that confirms their world will explode at any moment.

Trying to persuade a child at night that there are no monsters or kidnappers about to attack them is a Herculean task. Trying to do it on very little sleep, because they are waking all the time, is a particular form of torture!

The important thing to remember is that as the child or young person gains more skills, things will get better. As they grow and develop, they will become braver. Giving your child or young adult some additional skills can help along the way.

Appendix

Appendix 1: Template of the Worry-o-meter

Appendix 2: Creating the stairs

Use this design to make the stairs.

If you need more stairs, just add more in. Sometimes you may need to create a half-stair if the next stair was too difficult

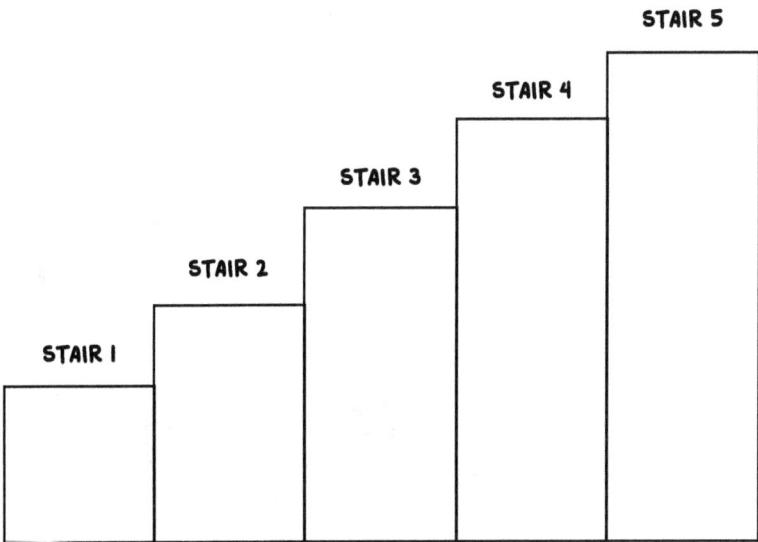

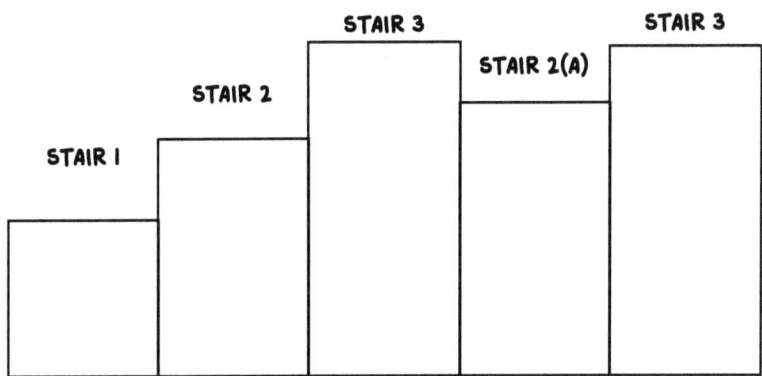

Appendix 3: The stairs towards success

Remember each stair is successful when it has been attempted. Sometimes the goal is not reached, and then some in-between stairs may need to be inserted. For instance, if Antonia could not lie in bed for 30 minutes, next time we would try for 10 minutes a few times, then keep working up the stairs.

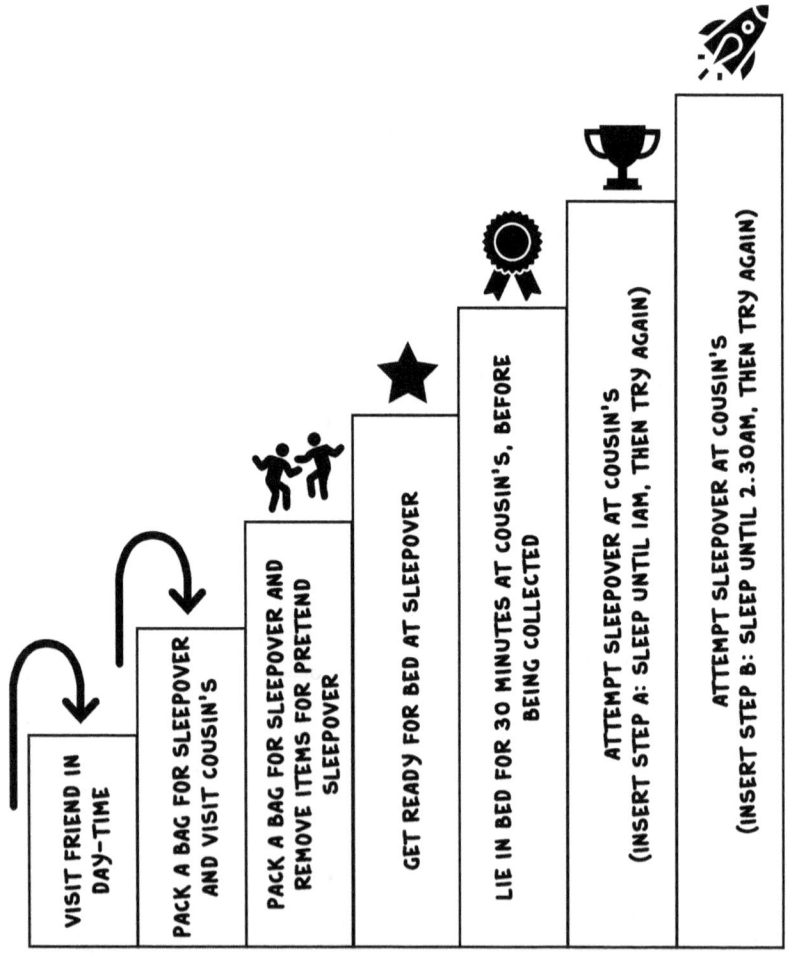

Useful Resources

USEFUL ONLINE RESOURCES

Beyond Blue

The Beyond Blue website is well known for anxiety and depression but there is also a Youth Beyond Blue website at **www.youthbeyondblue.com** which features anxiety

The BRAVE Program

The BRAVE Program is an interactive, online program for the prevention and treatment of childhood and adolescent anxiety. The programs are free, and provide ways for children and teenagers to better cope with their worries. There are also programs for parents.

https://brave4you.psy.uq.edu.au/

Cool Kids Online

An online research program for 7-12 year olds, which allows parents and children to work together to learn strategies to manage child anxiety

https://www.mq.edu.au/about/campus-services-and-facilities/hospital-and-clinics/centre-for-emotiional-health-clinic/prgrams-for-children-and-teenagers/online-treatment-accordions/cool-kids-online

Headspace

Headspace is run by the Australian National Youth Mental Health Foundation and provides early intervention mental health services to 12-25 year olds. It is a valuable source of support for older children and young adults.

https://headspace.org.au

Kids Helpline

Phone and real time web-based crisis support for youth (5-25 years)

http://www.kidshelp.com.au

Smiling Mind

A website and app teaching Mindfulness Meditation to young people (7 years up) with both Apple and Android apps available

http://smilingmind.com.au

REFERENCES AND OTHER USEFUL RESOURCES

Aisbett, Bev (1993): Living with "It": A survivor's guide to panic attacks. Australia: Angus and Robertson.

American Psychiatric Association, publisher; American Psychiatric Association. DSM-5 Task Force (2013): Diagnostic and statistical manual of mental disorders. DSM-5. Fifth edition. Arlington, Va.: American Psychiatric Association.

Attwood, Tony; Callesen, Kirsten; Moller-Nielsen, Annette (2008): THE CAT-Kit: Cognitive Affective Training Manual. Second Revised Edition. Arlington TX: Future Horizons.

Australian Government Department of Health (2015): Young Minds Matter: The second Australian Child and Adolescent Survey of Mental Health and Wellbeing. Available online at **https://youngmindsmatter.telethonkids.org.au/siteassets/media-docs---young-minds-matter/summarybookletweb.pdf**, updated on Dec 2017.

Australian Temperament Project (ATP). With assistance of Australian Institute of Family Studies, the Royal Children's Hospital, University of Melbourne and Deakin University. Available online at **http://www3.aifs.gov.au/atp/**.

Beesdo, K.; Knappe, S.; Pine, D. S. (2009): Anxiety and Anxiety Disorders in Children and Adolescents: Developmental issues and implications for DSM-V. In *Psychiatric Clinics of North America*

32 (3), pp. 483–524. Available online at **https://ncbi.nlm.nih.gov/pmc/articles/pmc3018839**, checked on 8/11/2017.

Dacey, John S.; Fiore, Lisa B. (2000): Your Anxious Child. How parents and teachers can relieve anxiety in children. San Francisco CA: Jossey Bass.

Donnelly, Kate Collins (2014): Starving the Anxiety Gremlin: A cognitive behavioural therapy workbook on anxiety management for children aged 5-9. London and Philadelphia: Jessica Kingsley Publishers.

Dweck, Carol (2017): Mindset: Changing the way you think to fulfil your potential. revised edition. London: Robinson.

Huebner, Dawn (2002): What to Do When You Dread Your Bed: A kid's guide to overcoming problems with sleep. Washington DC: Magination Press.

Huebner, Dawn (2006): What to Do When You Worry Too Much: A kid's guide to overcoming anxiety. Washington DC: Magination Press.

Innes, Shona (2016): Worries are Like Clouds: Bonnier Publishing Australia.

Ironside, Virginia (2011): The Huge Bag of Worries. GB: Hachette Children's Group.

Milrod, Barbara (2017): Child anxiety and parenting in the Trump era. The Conversation. Available online at (**https://theconversation.com/child-anxiety-and-parenting-in-the-trump-era-75979**).

Mischel, Walter; Ebbesen, Ebbe: and ,Raskoff Zeiss, Antonette (1972): Cognitive and Attentional Mechanisms in Delay of Gratification. In Journal of Personality and Social Psychology 21 (2), pp. 204–218.

Moffitt, Terrie E.; Arseneault, Louise; Belsky, Daniel; Dickson, Nigel; Hancox, Robert J.; Harrington, HonaLee et al. (2011): A gradient of childhood self-control predicts health, wealth, and public safety. In PNAS 108 (7), pp. 2693–2698. DOI: 10.1073/pnas.1010076108.

Moroney, Trace (2005): I'm Feeling Scared. Australia: Bonnier Publishing Australia.

Moses, Brian (1998): Your Feelings: I'm worried. GB: Hachette Children's Group.

Pass, L.; Mastroyannopoulou, K.; Coker, S.; Murray, L.; Dodd, H. (2017): Verbal Information Transfer in Real-Life: When Mothers Worry About Their Child Starting School. In *Journal of Child and Family Studies* 26 (8), pp. 2324–2334.

Rapee, Ronald (2000): Helping Your Anxious Child: A Step-by-Step Guide for Parents. Oakland, CA: New Harginger Publications Inc.

Rapee, Ronald: Lyneham, Heidi; Schniering, Carolyn; Wuthrich, Viviana; Abbott, Maree; Hudson, Jennifer and Wignall, Ann. Cool Kids Anxiety Program Kit (2006). Centre for Emotional Health, Macquarie University, Sydney.

Rapee, Ronald; Wignall, Ann; Spence, Susan; Cobham, Vanessa and Heidi Lyneham (2008): Helping Your Anxious Child:

A step-by-step guide for parents. 2nd edition. Oakland, CA: New Harbinger Publications Inc.

Sburlati, Elizabeth S.; Lyneham, Heidi J.; Schniering, Carolyn A.; Rapee, Ronald M. (2014): Evidence-Based CBT for Anxiety and Depression in Children and Adolescents: A Competencies Based Approach. Chichester, West Sussex, UK: John Wiley & Sons Ltd.

Service, Owain; Gallagher, Rory (2017): Think Small: The surprisingly simple ways to reach big goals. London: Michael O'Mara Books Limited.

The National Institute of Mental Health Information Resource Center (2001-2004): National Institute of Mental Health. Prevalence of Any Anxiety Disorder Among Adolescents. Available online at **https://www.nimh.nih.gov/health/statistics/any-anxiety-disorder.shtml**, updated on November 2017.

Van Steensel, Francisca J.A; Heeman Emma J. (2017): Anxiety Levels in Children with Autism Spectrum Disorder: A Meta-Analysis. In *Journal of Child and Family Studies* 26, pp. 1753–1767.

Waddell, Martin (2017): Owl Babies. GB: Walker Books Ltd.

I'm Scared

ACKNOWLEDGEMENTS

This book would not have been written without the encouragement and support of Dr Sonja Skocic, clinical psychologist, who suggested I had important things to say, and should publish a book. I give her hearty thanks for the enthusiasm and encouragement she has offered every step of the way.

A special thank you to Julie Postance who has helped me to understand the very complicated and nuanced art of writing and publishing a book. Her patience and warm support has been greatly appreciated.

The patience of my creative team of Aksaramantra from 99 Designs and Paul Cox from Upwork also cannot be underestimated. They persevered with me when I was struggling under time pressure and responded cheerily even when I am sure they had had enough.

I thank Aksaramantra for the brilliant cover designs, and Paul for the wonderful cartoons, and both for showing such patience in adapting them according to my wishes. Enormous thanks, also, to Sophie White for her extremely valuable advice, assistance and patience with final layout and design.

There is an art to taking a good photograph, especially when the subject doesn't like to be photographed. Phil Nitchie from Nitch Photography, has a great ability to make the subject feel comfortable, and to create brilliant designs. Thanks Phil!

To Vanessa Wing-Quay, Colin McMeekin and Adam Velcek, my readers and supporters through my working life, along with Robyn, Pam and Alison, I thank you. Special appreciation and thanks go to Elizabeth Williams for her kind words in the Foreword.

It is always wonderful to have a good editor, and I greatly appreciate the work of Amanda Spedding who has helped me navigate this path. Also, the great work done by Cruzialdesigns who has helped with the layout of this book. Not an easy task.

I acknowledge the incredible work done by Professor Ronald Rapee from Macquarie University, who has produced excellent work throughout his career in this field. I greatly valued his first edition of *Helping Your Anxious Child*, when beginning work in this field, and the second edition — in collaboration with others — has been equally helpful and hugely successful.

His work has been inspirational, and the reader is referred to his excellent book for a step-by-step, evidence-based program, along with the Cool Kids programs produced by Macquarie University.

Other excellent work which has been inspirational, has been the work by Professor Tony Attwood, in relation to anxious children with Autism Spectrum Disorder, and Professor Paula Barrett who first pioneered the FRIENDS and FRIENDS for life programs.

Finally, to my parents and family, the greatest vote of thanks for all your encouragement through life. Thanks especially goes to Ruth for her valuable editor's eye, and for her invaluable suggestions.

www.ingramcontent.com/pod-product-compliance
Lightning Source LLC
Chambersburg PA
CBHW061643040426
42446CB00010B/1558